Thrive Through Tears

anyway

Misty VanderWeele

©2015 Misty VanderWeele
ISBN 978-0-9893247-3-1
Cover Design by Misty VanderWeele
Cover Photography by Relic Photographic, Wasilla, Alaska

All rights reserved. Printed in the United States of America. No part of this publication may be reproduced, stored in a retrieval system, or transmitted in any form or by means electronic, mechanical, photocopied, or otherwise without written permission from publisher.

Publisher, Misty VanderWeele (MV International) PO Box 4124 Palmer, Alaska 99645

This book is designed for self-help and inspirational purposes. It is distributed with the understanding that the publisher is not engaged in the dispensation of legal, psychological, or any other professional or medical advice. Further the publisher shall not be held liable to any person or entity for any incidental or consequential damages caused directly or indirectly.

When life tries to break you; this book is for you.

Acknowledgments

First and foremost I'd like to bow down and thank our creator and my God. I am so deeply humbled by your love for me. I can finally rest knowing my boy is safe, dancing, and disease free. These words help guide me: *"God grant me the serenity to accept the things I cannot change, the courage to change the things I can, and the wisdom to know the difference."*

Next, my daughter, Jenna. Thank you for living from your heart in all that you do and especially loving me and wanting me to be in your life. Without your support and our mother/daughter connection this book and all that I do would not be possible.

To the incredible man I married. You've told me that as long as I'm at your side you will have strength; well, Glen, this goes both ways. Thank you for the confidence you have in me. It carries me through all the self-doubt and helps me see there is more to life than feeling sad over the loss of our Luke.

My beautiful sister Autee Tweedy, thank you for always being here for me. It's been an adjustment with you moving so far away but just know that you have an uncanny way of knowing right when I need you the most. Your encouragement and support I treasure. Also, thank you for being the most wonderful aunt to my kids.

To ALL sides of my family, including all my cousins, aunts, and in-laws. Thank you for loving me, for caring for me, for supporting me through my mother's grief. Without you my life wouldn't have the meaning that it does.

To the Duchenne Community, thank you for supporting me when Luke was alive, and an even bigger thank you for your continued support now that he has transcended to Heaven. Without you, none of what I do would be possible. Please know that I am here if you ever need me.

Duchenne Muscular Dystrophy, I can't say that I like you very much, but I can thank you for all the life lessons you've taught me. You've made me stronger; you've made me more sincere just as much as you've tried to take me down. I want you to know you have not won. Because I know death is a part of life, just as much as you can't have light if there was only darkness. I've made peace with you, that is why I can continue on. So again, thank you for your life lessons. I wouldn't be who I am without you. Further, this book would not have been possible.

Cindy Atkins, from Angels At My Door. Thank you for the beautiful work you do. You have helped enrich my mother's grief journey. You have helped, whether you know it or not, in bringing this book to fruition. Your support and friendship is greatly appreciated.

Liza Collins, although we've only known each other for a few months: thank you for following your gut in reaching out to me. Your guided meditation helped bring me focus and drove home, without a doubt, that our loved ones who have passed may not be here in the physical sense but they are very much here in spirit. I'm excited to see what the future holds for you and me.

Next, to my most awesome editor. Without her services, view on life, and timely professional manner, the last few books wouldn't have happened when they did. Thank you Lucia Craven of Craven Review, like I said in my book *Heart Shaped Rocks* I always knew you'd turn out to be an incredible individual. How wonderful it is to be working with you.

To my beloved partner in crime, my forever guardian angel, Luke my son. Thank you so much for the continued presence in my life. The signs you send never cease to amaze me. No, we can't sit down and have a conversation or see each other; although my humanness craves this, my soul knows two things. One, we can still have a relationship; it just looks and feels different. And two, I will see you again. I will always bask in the continuance of our unbreakable sacred connection.

Table of Contents

Thrive Through Tears; anyway.

   INTRODUCTION...11

In Your Face Duchenne Muscular Dystrophy, All Pain, All GLORY! (The Beginning)..14

   FOREWORD..15
      Preface by Debra Miller..18
   INTRODUCTION...21
      Hold On..21
   CHAPTER ONE..22
      Where's Luke?..22
      Nagging Feeling..24
      Hide-and-Go-Seek..24
      Medical Journal...25
      Mom on a Mission...25
      Clown Mobile...26
      Family Meeting..26
      Fetal Position...27
      Light Bulb Question...27
      Where Did This Come From..28
   CHAPTER TWO...29
      One Foot In Front Of The Other................................29
      Max 31
      Dawn of the TIGER..32
      You're Stuck With Us..32
      You Are My Sunshine..33
      Gene Therapy Trials..33
      On a Wing and a Prayer...34
      Good Will Ambassador..35
      Long Way Home...36
   CHAPTER THREE..38
      I Can Heal My Life...38
      Wheelbarrow...40
      Ms. Sped Bus..40
      Bath Tub Fun..41

    The Luke Sled 42
    Give me 5 + 1 42
    Grandma with the White Chevy Truck 43
CHAPTER FOUR 45
    Freedom 45
    Call From The School Nurse 46
    Blessing in Disguise 47
    Cherish These Days 49
    Here Comes Santa Claus 50
    Human Pancake 51
    Shiny Penny 51
    Alaskan Outdoor Fun 52
    Close Call 53
    Fifth Grade Field Trip 54
CHAPTER FIVE 56
    Every Life is Precious 56
    Brother and Sister 58
    Hand Bell Hell 59
    Stephanie 60
    Lesson in Water Safety 60
    Secret Christmas Project 61
    All of The Above 62
CHAPTER SIX 65
    All About Luke 65
    Luke's New Hero 66
    Social Isolation 67
    Down To The Bone 68
    Run For Our Sons 71
    Possibilities 73
    Buggy Time 73
    Another Surgery 74
    Steven 75
    Sweet 16 76
    To Give up or FIGHT, that is the question 76
    Jenna Benna 77
    You Might Be a Red Neck If 79
    Luke's Bump 80
    Jello Shooters 81
    It wasn't long enough 81

CHAPTER SEVEN..84
   Life Goes On...84
   Yard Work...86
   Hell And Back..86
   Don't Die Without Me..87
   Hospital Blessing..88
   My Doggie..91
   Class Ring..91
   Advocating...92
   This Place...92
   Let There Be Light..94
CHAPTER EIGHT..95
   I Did It..98
   Eyes Like Saucers...99
   Superman Syndrome..100
   I Need Your Help..101
   Let's Do it Right Here...101
   One Stressed Out Mama...102

Three Books In One...104

INTRODUCTION...106
   Preface...109
CHAPTER ONE: THE HEART OF THE MATTER..........................111
   God wouldn't give me more than I could handle............111
   "You're pregnant."...112
   Little Bird...112
   "Are you okay?"..113
   Cheerio O's..114
   Whirlwind..114
   Furniture to Furniture..114
   Brotherly Love..115
   Road Kill..115
   Shared Custody..115
CHAPTER TWO: HAVE A HEART...116
   He Found His Way Back to Her..117
   Brownies..118
   Caregiver Nightmare..119
   Her Gift..119
   Pirates of the Caribbean..120
   Tinkerbelle Café..121

    It Stresses Me Out!...*121*
    The Heart in My Pocket..*121*
    Glasses...*122*
    Peace Teacher..*122*
    No More Bread..*123*
   CHAPTER THREE: LOVE ROCKS......................................*125*
    Don't Die Without Me...*125*
    In Your Face Duchenne Muscular Dystrophy.................*126*
    She Got Her Hug..*126*
    Victory Bible Camp...*127*
    Mom, Look!..*127*
   CHAPTER FOUR: BIG HEARTED.......................................*128*
    Lego Nation..*129*
    Gold Mine Conversation..*129*
    "Was I wanted?"..*130*
    Middle School Blossom..*130*
    Orange Crush...*131*
    Home Again..*131*
    Her Babies..*132*
    13th Birthday..*132*
    Walks with Luke...*133*
    Love at First Sight...*133*
   CHAPTER FIVE: THE HEART WITHIN.............................*134*
    Keeping House...*135*
    Beach Dream..*135*
    Cloudy Cold Day..*135*
    For My Brother..*136*
   EPILOGUE: LIVING LIFE THROUGH JENNA-COLORED
GLASSES...*136*

Thrive Through Tears; anyway..................

    Something Was Off..*138*
    "Are you ready to go to heaven?".....................................*139*
    They Lined the Halls...*139*
    Wait for Me..*140*
    Lock of Hair...*140*
    Driving Home..*141*
    Let Others Take Care of You...*141*
    Non Essential Angels..*142*
    Cards, Flowers, Gifts..*142*

500 Candles..142
Luke's Place..143
The Year of Firsts..144
Letters to Luke..145
Little Bird...145
Grief Isn't a Part of My Personality................147
Unbreakable Connection...............................147
"Mom it's okay, I'm right here, you got this." ...148
Luke Days...150
Embracing Mother's Grief............................150
I am doing it..151

Love Story within a Love Story..........................
   WHO IS MISTY VANDERWEELE...........................153

Thrive Through Tears; anyway

Introduction

Time, once given, isn't something you can ever get back. The fact that you are spending some of yours with me to read *Thrive Through Tears; anyway* deeply humbles me. I don't take it lightly. Please accept my sincere thank you.

I come from a place I couldn't even fathom not long ago. A place of fighting in agony to surrender, and onward since my beloved son, Luke, ascended to heaven at the young age of 21, from an impacted, twisted colon. The disease Duchenne Muscular Dystrophy had made his body too weak to fight or even withstand surgery – a surgery he was opposed to anyway.

Before Luke passed I viewed his life as a Sacred Journey of Unknown Length of Time. It is, if you think about it, the same journey that each and every one of us finds ourselves on. However, I wasn't consciously aware of this fact until Luke was diagnosed at age 4. Not only did they tell me that Luke had Duchenne Muscular Dystrophy, an incurable muscle disease that would rob him of physical independence, they said he would not survive into adulthood.

I say "consciously" because at the time I was an upside down butterfly trying to find her way in a turbulent gust of being a single mom. But when Luke was diagnosed I somehow grabbed the reins of my life and started to gain more control. I was not perfect, mind you, but much more sane, which was strange, since the devastation of hearing what every parent dreads was gut ripping. Learning that your child will die after a disease ravages his body, but not his mind, and that there isn't anything you can do is like no other lesson. It sent me into a fetal position for a week. I couldn't even drive. My entire body ached. I remained stricken until I was asked a question that changed the course of my life. You see, Luke's life gave me the gift of purpose and mission. It became my identity even through the agonizing and ongoing grief, as Duchenne took from him every day. His life, his sacred journey, is one I'd do all over again in a heartbeat if only it wasn't so selfish. Duchenne made Luke's life so hard. I wouldn't ask that of him. Luke was not only my son, he was my friend.

This book is really three books in one. *In Your Face Duchenne Muscular Dystrophy, All Pain All Glory* is the story of Luke's first 18 years on this planet. Published in 2010, it details how he lived in the face of his own death. *Heart Shaped Rocks: Don't Die Without Me* is the story of his sister, Jenna. Published in 2014, it details how she lived knowing that one day he would die, and how she went on when he did. *Thrive Through Tears; anyway* A Mothers Grief Revised is the final book that completes the framework of where I stand before, during, and after my son's passing.

The three books encompass a life journey of tremendous love, hope, determination, continuous heartbreak, grief beyond comprehension, the insufferable pain of loss, and the cherished mystery of life.

Finally, this book is about my commitment to Thrive Through Tears anyway. It's about my commitment to live, despite the agonizing grief of witnessing a horrible disease hurt my son over and over, and despite the shock of Luke's passing and the year of "firsts" missing him. To arrive finally at a space of grieving and surrendering grace. And ultimately the signs and "ah-ha" moments that got me here. It is a story for anyone who has lost a child.

In Your Face Duchenne Muscular Dystrophy, All Pain, All GLORY! (The Beginning)

FOREWORD

In Your Face is a true life journey of tremendous love, hope, continuous heart break, silent pain and the cherished mystery of life. A candid story that is both the worst and the best thing that has ever happened to me. A story of transformation that started when my son, Luke, was only four years old.

On a sunny Alaskan July day, life as I knew it changed in nine words. Words that no parent should ever have to hear. Words I'll never forget: "I am sorry. Your son has Duchenne Muscular Dystrophy." The pain was deafening in my ears; my entire world was spinning. My mind was screaming NO! Not my little boy! In an instant I went from dreams of sports, bicycles, outdoor hunting and fishing, snowmobiling and most of the outdoor Alaskan lifestyle, to living in the face of the possibility of my son's early death.

If you have ever watched the Jerry Lewis MDA Labor Day Telethon, you have heard of Duchenne Muscular Dystrophy or (DMD). DMD, or just Duchenne as I like to call it, is the most common life- threatening form Muscular Dystrophy (MD) and is often confused with MS. Duchenne is considered a genetic muscle wasting disorder. Typically, Duchenne boys are diagnosed before age five. They noticeably fatigue easily and find it challenging keeping up with others their age as their muscles swell and joints become restricted. The simplest of tasks like holding a pencil or rolling over in bed become difficult and eventually impossible. Most Duchenne boys need a wheelchair between ages of 10-12. As they get older and Duchenne progresses, the heart and breathing muscles become compromised and begin to fail. Sadly, most boys with Duchenne have not survived their teens. Duchenne affects about one in 3,500 boys, with nearly 20,000 born each year around the world.

Duchenne is caused by a gene mutation on the X chromosome, and that is why the disease almost exclusively affects males. Females have two X chromosomes, so if the Duchenne-causing mutation occurs in one, the other compensates for the fault. Women carry the defective gene but almost never manifest the symptoms to a deadly degree. Carriers have a 50 percent chance of passing along the defective gene to their male offspring and since males don't have another X chromosome to compensate for the fault, they develop the disease. The daughters of carrier women have a 25 percent chance of being carriers themselves.

Those with Duchenne appear normal at birth but are usually confined to a wheelchair by their early teens as the disease progresses. At the time of Luke's diagnosis over 14 years ago before the internet, I was told that Duchenne boys usually pass away during their teen years. The last few years, however, that outlook has changed somewhat as many Duchenne boys are living several years longer, some even into their early 30s.

My son Luke is now 18 and is considered to be in the last phase of the disease because he is in a wheelchair full time and requires respiratory and cardiac therapy.

I have gone from, "Why God why?" to, "Thank you Luke for honoring me in choosing me as your mother." I believe that each and every one of us choose our parents before being born here on this planet. It is the only explanation that makes sense to me, because in my book no loving God would make or cause this sort of pain in anyone's life especially that of a little child.

The one thing that stands fast is that, although Luke hasn't been cured, he has lived longer than "they" told me he would. There have been times that I thought I would die from the pain of it all and times of complete and utter bliss. The many angels who have crossed our path in the form of teachers, journalists, doctors, nurses, therapists, family, friends, care providers and complete strangers I wouldn't have known otherwise. Life is such a mystery and I don't want to miss any of it!

I am writing In Your Face during Luke's senior year in high school as a gift to him for graduation. I think completing 12 years of education is an accomplishment for any 18-year-old, but especially for a Duchenne boy who has triumphed in the face of death. I am writing it as a way to preserve the essence of our sacred journey of unknown length together. To have something tangible that will go on and help others long after his passage to heaven. With that being said, now I know why parents write memoirs after their children pass. I had no idea about the amount of energy writing would take and the emotion I would expend while still living every day and providing Luke care and sound advice so that he is able to go on and advocate for himself and deal with his medical condition.

When I sat down to write this book, I realized that I remembered the past in sort of a dream-like consciousness. I don't know if we all remember our pasts like this or whether my memory is trying to help me distance myself from the horror of watching my boy's body being ravaged by Duchenne. I thought long and hard about how I was going to be able to tell my story in an uplifting positive way without being consumed by the pain as I relived the good, the bad and the ugly imprint Duchenne has tried to force upon me. I especially want to make sure I convey how I have had to change my internal belief system and the way I perceived everything about who I am and about life in general to not only survive, but thrive. My entire mission is to weave what is a very sad human circumstance into threads of hope to inspire a Duchenne Movement. People not knowing that 20,000 boys a year are being diagnosed with Duchenne, which some have considered a death sentence, is not acceptable!

Since memory comes back to us in flashes of conversations, tidbits of recollection and the emotional impact that past events have upon us, instead of one continuous thread, I started each chapter with a titled introduction, then titled memory segments that follow Luke's progression of Duchenne. Eventually ending with an entire chapter dedicated to anyone who is touched by Duchenne wanting to join the Duchenne Movement or at least wear the t-shirt. You can find out more about me and pick up a free guide for "THRIVING" In-The-Face of Duchenne at http://MistyVanderweele.com.

Some of the names have been changed as some of the issues and challenges often involved a group of individuals and not always in the most positive of ways. I am extremely happy that I was able to use a lot of real names, as many of the people in this story have been very supportive. Many heartfelt tears have been shed during the creation of this book and I wouldn't change that for the world. After all life is meant to be felt and lived!

From the beginning I, like every other mother out there, didn't want to miss one smile, one tear, one struggle, or one triumph of my child's life. What other choice does a mother have when the reality of her child's probable death is so IN YOUR FACE?

Preface by Debra Miller

The very first book of the Bible depicts a story about Abraham's nephew, Lot, who was kidnapped by the enemy. When Abram (Abraham) heard that his nephew had been taken captive, he called out his army of trained men and went in pursuit. During the night Abram attacked the enemy. He recovered all the goods and brought back his nephew, Lot and ALL his possessions. (Genesis chapter 14:14-14:16)

In Your Face is a story about a remarkable young man, Luke, the love of his mother and the call to action that is the result of her love and her faith. It's a safe assumption that Abraham was in constant prayer with God, but he didn't stop there. He also took action and stepped out in faith to save his nephew. Misty VanderWeele is building a different kind of "army," an army of parents, patients and advocates who aren't content to let others decide the future for those they love who are afflicted with Duchenne muscular dystrophy.

The small town in Alaska where Luke and Misty live is about as isolated as you can get from the hubs of science and support groups. Perhaps Misty's self-reliance is enhanced by this distance since she had to find her own way in dealing with Duchenne. Whatever the cause, Misty sets an example for all families that have had their dreams for their child's future shattered. She did not shelter her son from living a full life; in fact, Luke has had the benefit of the great outdoors and is getting ready for college next year.

None of us really knows what we are capable of until the need arises. If we get lulled into thinking that the "experts" will take care of our children, then we are short changing our children and ourselves by not experiencing the deep satisfaction that comes with knowing we are working toward the solution. Those who have taken action, whether it be local fund raising or advocacy, have started a chain reaction of events and contacts that will move us much closer to a cure for Duchenne.

When our son was diagnosed with Duchenne seven years ago, we knew that this disease was much bigger than we were and that our son was truly in God's hands. We noticed a tendency among some other DMD parents we met to put their faith in people they believed had the answers, whether it be organizations, science or medicine. But as Abraham showed, God gives us opportunities to act and help others.

In Your Face is a perfect title for this book. Misty has taken the gloves off and has posed a challenge to everyone to be part of the cure for Duchenne. She is a perfect example of a mom who has recognized the power of the individual and she offers solutions and encouragement to families everywhere. Very few people ever hear the word Duchenne until someone close to them is diagnosed. Until the public knows about this disease, it will remain underfunded for research and care. Misty knows this and is stepping outside the box to get the word out about Duchenne.

We don't know what the future holds for our boys that have Duchenne, but we do know that everyone affected with this disease has a responsibility to contribute what they can to change the outcome. Everyone has something to add. Misty didn't train to be an author, but when she saw the need she rose to the occasion.

Misty and Luke's journey is an extraordinary story of love, determination and bravery. If Misty had analyzed her experience and skill set to determine if, or what, she should do to help boys with Duchenne, it's very possible she'd still be pondering that list. She realized that there just wasn't enough time to do that, and she took the first step. When you read this book, I hope you will be as inspired as I am by Misty's determination.

To Misty, with gratitude from another parent of a boy with Duchenne,

    Debra Miller
    President and Founder
    CureDuchenne

Introduction

Hold On

What would you do if you were told your child would die from a life threatening incurable disease, but before death came your child would require a wheelchair to walk and depend on someone else to provide all their physical needs, that living into adulthood most likely wasn't going to happen? That there wasn't anything you could do about it. But, here take this card and contact the Jerry Lewis Muscular Dystrophy Association.

Would you keel over and die yourself from the pure agony of it; would you go down to the bar and drink your sorrows away. Would you pray like you have never prayed before? Would you convince yourself that "they" are doing everything they can to find a cure? Or, would it be your "wake up call" to face all and even more than you think you can be?

Further how would you write about something that has ripped your heart out too many times to count, at the same time given you a voice of inspiration?

Fasten your seat belt and hold on, because you're about to find out.

Chapter One

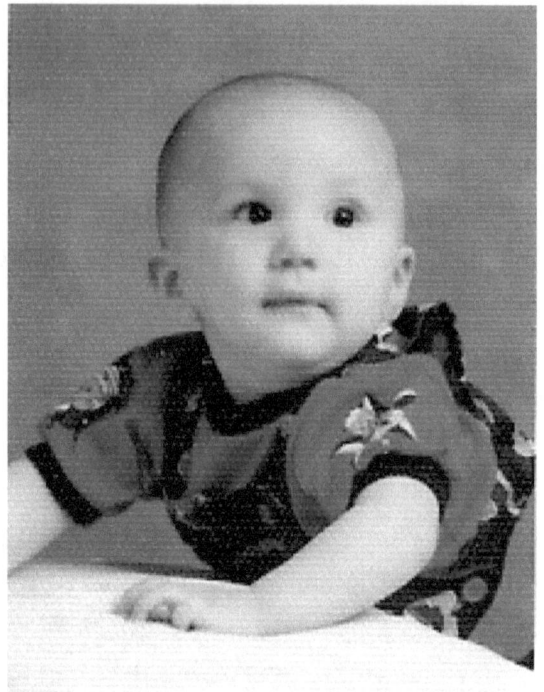

Little Luke (6 months) 1992

Picture taken before we had any idea the word Duchenne even existed. This very year Luke won a beautiful baby contest. I remember thinking how incredible it was to have a beautiful, healthy son.

Where's Luke?

Luke was born a healthy bouncing baby boy on December 22 1991. What better gift to receive than a baby for Christmas? Luke's father Pat shed large hot tears that landed on my arm when he first laid eyes on his son. The hospital gave us a giant Christmas stocking to take him home in and I still have the pictures of Luke in the stocking under the Christmas tree.

Now every time I think of Luke's birth, I think of the bible verse "Through him you shall know me." For I have come closer than most to the true knowing of the spirit through watching my son face his mortality much sooner than any of us feel comfortable with.

My relationship with Luke's dad was rocky before we married and worsened over time. In a one month time span we were married, miscarried our first child and my dad died. All of these are huge stresses for any relationship, not to mention for kids of only 19. We officially divorced when Luke was two and we have always shared joint physical custody. Luke spends pretty much equal amounts of time at each home. He often says he is the luckiest kid around because he has two parents who love him, two bedrooms, two incredible stepparents, two sisters, two brothers and a family so large that we have to rent the local borough gym for birthday parties.

The first time I had any inkling that there might be something wrong with Luke was when a childcare provider who had special needs children of her own told us that she noticed Luke was not as strong as he should be and that he seemed overly cautious about doing anything physical like the swings or walking up and down stairs. My immediate reaction was anger. "There was nothing wrong with my child." I took him to a program called "Child Find" to get him evaluated so that I could prove her wrong. But Luke wouldn't participate in any of the physical tests at all. As I looked around at the other children breezing through the tests, I knew that Luke couldn't perform most of what I as seeing. It was so "In My Face." I can still remember my throat tightening and those first threatening feelings of nausea in the pit of my stomach that would soon become the norm. Somewhere in the back of my mind I knew but I wasn't ready to face it. I quickly pressed the feeling down.

Nagging Feeling

I knew I had to find a doctor and I wanted the very best pediatrician Alaska had to offer. At the time, Alaska's total state population was just over 603,000 and the closest and largest hospital in the state was over an hour and a half away. It was also 1996, just before the internet became the rage that it is today. I had to find a doctor using the old-fashioned Yellow Pages phone book.

The pediatrician I wanted was on vacation but I went ahead and made the appointment anyway. I needed to find out what was going on with my son. More and more "little things" kept taking me back to the same spot. Little things like Luke standing at the top of a long steep staircase crying for my help. This behavior might be normal for a one year old, but definitely not for a 4 year old.

Luke was examined for a long time and pretty soon, every kid-doctor on staff at the hospital that day was in the room. I have come to learn over the years that this is never a good sign. They all agreed that Luke was a little small for his age and that he was slower than the average 4 year old. They all said they were pretty sure that he would catch up in a year or two. But just to be on the safe side I was to bring Luke back in year. I, being a young mom with my first child, accepted with relief what I was being told.

Hide-and-Go-Seek

Kids were running all around playing hide-and-go-seek. They were having a blast! When I realized I hadn't seen Luke for some time, I started looking for him. I almost started to panic when I spotted him sitting on a mound of grass. I remember stopping in my tracks and feeling sort of sick inside. He was happy and had a smile on his face but he wasn't participating with the other children. This bothered me big time. I knew something had to be wrong, but I just didn't know what.

Medical Journal

My mom brought over her trusty medical journal with the bad news. The journal described exactly the symptoms my son was having: waddling gait when walking, hard time getting up from the floor, large calf muscles, protruding abdomen. My breath caught in my throat. The sickening feeling in my stomach which was becoming all too familiar, that I had pushed down so many times before, rolled in my gut. I struggled with what I was reading as my mind still wanted to hang onto the idea that everything was fine. After all, my mom was one of 5 sisters who all had healthy boys including my brother. But I knew I had to find out the answers to my burning questions. What was wrong with my little boy? Why wasn't he a monkey? Why didn't he run? Why was he scared to go up and down stairs? Why did he cry and whine all the time?

Mom on a Mission

Enough was enough. I was out for blood by this point. I wasn't going to stop pushing ahead until I found out exactly what was going on with Luke. This time I was going to find the pediatrician I wanted in the first place. I wanted a full blood panel done. I wanted answers.

Dr. Bloodwork (named changed for confidentiality reasons) examined Luke and his face was serious. He not only agreed that we needed to do Luke's blood work, he wanted an additional blood test done to measure the CK, or the creatine kinase levels, in his blood. If you have extremely elevated CK levels you might have muscular dystrophy.

By the time Luke and I got home a couple of hours later, there was message from Dr. Bloodwork telling us that Luke's dad and I were to come in the next day, which was a Saturday. He also said to make sure that someone else could drive us. No way around it, this was bad news. The message left me barely breathing. I was whirling inside and scared out of my mind! That Friday night was the first of many sleepless nights.

Clown Mobile

I stared at the laughing clown with large curly orange hair swinging from the ceiling, waiting, waiting, waiting. I thought, "Damn when was the doctor coming in!" I felt like I was going to vomit. I knew it was bad news, but I was still holding on to the very small hope that everything was fine. When the blow of what the doctor said sank in, the room started to spin and voices sounded like they were coming from a tunnel. I am not even sure how I walked out of the hospital. I was floating, suffocating, spinning off balance. I remember I felt like I had no legs. I remember Luke's father and my cousin who drove us. I remember feeling relieved that it wasn't my week to have Luke. I couldn't face him yet. How could I? What was I going to do? How was I going to survive?

Family Meeting

I have a very large and local family so I thought it was imperative that I call a family meeting. I wanted to let everyone know about the diagnosis and I only wanted to have to tell the story once. I remember my cousin driving us to the meeting about 30 minutes away. The trees blurred by as we drove. I felt like there was a hurricane of turmoil raging in side of me, threatening to break me in two!

The first person I saw when I walked in was my mother. The other faces were not in focus. As my mother held me up in her arms, the sound that came out of me was a primal call from one mother to the next. The only thing I could say was, "Its bad mamma!" over and over.

My grandma came to stay with me that night and it was a great comfort to have her there with me. I awoke in the middle of the night to her quietly crying out to God. I laid there and listened to her but I was numb. Everything felt like one big nightmare.

Fetal Position

There are no words to describe exactly what the first week of knowing my son had Duchenne Muscular Dystrophy was like. The shock. The grief of lost dreams I once had for my son. I lay in a fetal position for hours on end, weeping, pleading, begging to whom or what I couldn't tell you. I rehashed my situation a million times, always coming to the same outcome. I had to get my life in order. Time to grow up! Time to get past the divorce and time to end relationships that didn't serve me or Luke's highest good. It was high time I pull up the boot straps and love the shit out of my boy! Whatever time I had left with him. I knew it was going to take "ALL" of me. That which does not kill you only makes you stronger, right? Well, I was going to find out.

Light Bulb Question

Sitting at my grandfather's glass kitchen table, feeling numb from head to toe, I was spent from all the crying and grieving, not really knowing which way to go. My Aunt Kendra asked me why I thought this was happening and I said, "So I can help other people," as if I had always known the answer. Somehow I knew I had to turn these lemons I had been dealt into something positive, not only for me but for my little boy. The bills had to get paid and life still had to go on. It was up to me now. My life depended on it and Luke depended on it!

Where Did This Come From

The week after we knew that Luke had Duchenne, my mom, Luke and I all went in to have our genetic blood testing done. Luke needed a formal diagnosis and my mom and I needed to find out if we were carriers. I already knew in my heart that my mother wasn't a carrier and I was. I don't know how I knew, I just knew.

The blood work confirmed what I already knew. I was a carrier and my mother was not. After the initial wave of guilt washed over me, I felt relieved. I finally knew why my boy was different. I was sad because I felt that having more children was out of the question for me. I was crushed that my boy had a guaranteed struggle ahead of him. Some part of my brain immediately realized that my beloved son would most likely die from Duchenne Muscular Dystrophy.

Chapter Two

Luke, Summer 1997

Luke was 5 years old here.
He couldn't climb up on the tractor,
Glen had to lift him up there. I love how
he seems to be looking forward to
the future and the rest of his life.
He looks very happy.

One Foot In Front Of The Other

I felt a deep urgency to provide an excellent quality of life for my son because of the short life expectancy that is part of the Duchenne diagnosis. I refused to look at the negative for long. Somehow I found the strength to immediately take action and I started to read everything I could get my hands on about Duchenne. Even self-help books to better myself as a woman and a mother. I got in touch with the Muscular Dystrophy Association and Parent Project Muscular Dystrophy. Every time I faced another issue with the progression of Duchenne, I would push back harder and only let myself be overwrought with emotion in bit size pieces. I would dig deep, ask questions and hold fast to the idea of what was actually the best for Luke rather than what the doctors and other people told me to do. I also knew out of every bad thing, good happens. My life was living proof of that.

Something wonderful started to happen almost simultaneously during this early phase of our new life with Duchenne. My personal life took a turn for the better and romance was in the air. I was falling for my good friend Glen, who I think actually fell in love with Luke first. Which led me to moving to one of the most beautiful places in Alaska, VanderWeele Farms, which was owned by Glen's family. It seemed like fate to me because I was actually born in a car parked in the driveway of the main house at VanderWeele Farms some 26 years before!

The farm is a scenic magical place surrounded by magnificent power of the Alaskan mountains and had a way of helping to heal the gaping hole that had been dug into my heart by Duchenne. When I have a bad day, all I have to do is look outside or take a walk, breath in and let the peaceful power take over.

I found myself living a life that I hadn't even dreamed of with a man who totally "got" me. I still marvel over the fact that Glen chose a life with Luke and me, knowing full well it was a guaranteed heartache. However I truly believe there are no accidents and that I am meant to be living this life.

Every time I have faced a life-altering event and asked for a sign on what to do, I have received it, from what to do about Glen, the birth of my daughter and even Luke. I immediately started Luke on physical therapy but Luke's dad Pat and I decided against steroids. At the time everything I was reading about the long term use of steroids pointed out that steroids would lead to cataracts, diabetes, behavior issues, osteoporosis, cessation of growth, would also stunt puberty and "may" help with longer ambulation and "may" help with respiratory health. This wasn't good enough for me. I felt, why give Luke more problems to deal with? Doesn't he have enough problems already? Besides, there was not enough evidence at the time to prove to me that steroids actually helped Duchenne boys walk longer or improved their respiratory function.

Now, 13 years later, there is strong evidence that steroids can help improve some of the symptoms of Duchenne. However, should for me the use of steroids is a very personal one and only be considered for a quality of life and what is best for your child.

Max

Life had dealt me a huge challenge. I knew I had to make a change but I was scared to death for not only Luke's future but my own. The dance steps had been changed but I didn't know the dance. Plus Glen and my relationship was still very new. Even though I wanted to get married, I wanted Glen to be 100% sure that Luke and I were what he wanted. I was not interested in "shacking-up". However in lieu of my unique situation with Luke. Glen and I decided we would finish his little farm house he had been building, together. Enroll Luke into preschool and just see how we managed.

Luke, Glen and I moved in. I started working on the farm and the next natural thing that happened was to get Luke every little boy's dream. A puppy seemed a perfect fit. I grabbed at the "normalness." Anything to distance myself from the fact that Luke's childhood wasn't normal or what I had always dreamed of for him. I thought that giving Luke a companion was a great idea.

We picked up the cutest floppy eared puppy with a mask of a husky. Luke decided to name him Max.

Dawn of the TIGER

"ROAR" came a noise out from under the mat that was stood up in the shape of a tent. Our physical therapist, who was in the tent, yelled "NO, DON'T EAT ME!" On all fours, Luke came out roaring like a big tiger and they both laughed and rolled around on the floor. Luke's first experience with physical therapy at the age of 4 was such great fun. I am so thankful for that now. Luke loves physical therapy to this day and actually looks forward to it.

You're Stuck With Us

I think Luke was born a "motor head" with a Hotwheels car in his hand. I would find cars stuffed into every nook and cranny of his car seat and toddler bed. He would wake up with tire imprints on his face. He got his first mini 3 wheeler at the age of 3, then moved on to a 4-wheeler and rode it until he couldn't physically get on the thing.

By the time he was 4, Luke could tell you the make of every vehicle that was on the road without ever getting one wrong. That's probably the real reason my Glen, a motor head himself, fell in love with Luke, but don't tell him I told you that. The three of us were heading down the road, playing the Chevy, Ford, Dodge, Toyota game when Luke told Glen that he was stuck with us. Glen looked at me and said that was all right by him. That was the moment that I knew Glen was my man.

You Are My Sunshine

Luke and I went from sharing the same bedroom for 3 years to him having his very own "Big Boy" room when we moved in with Glen. Luke was only five and the night separation from me was a very hard transition for him to make. I would put him in bed and then the screaming and crying would start. Luke would cry "I don't want to go to bed" or "I need a drink of water" or "I need to go pee." He would work himself up into a frenzy of a sweating frightened boy. After yelling at him, pleading with him and trying to ignore him, I would get up and go into his room and hold him and sing his favorite song, "You Are My Sunshine." He would settle down but the minute I walked out, he would start in again. Glen and I would lay in bed at a loss for what to do for him. A few weeks into the behavior he started hollering, "Mommy save me!" It was so heartbreaking and I would say "Yes Luke, I will save you." Later Luke's plea turned into a simple request of "Save me." This ripped my heart out!

These night fits lasted for months. I was pretty sure he didn't understand about Duchenne and that he was just trying to get attention. I was at my wit's end with it until one night I wasn't going to take it anymore. I grabbed the "Happy Spoon" and the kitchen timer and walked into his room, looked him in the eye and stated, "I am going to set the timer for 15 minutes, so cry, kick, scream, do whatever you want for 15 minutes, but when this timer goes off, I want silence! If you continue to scream I am going to spank your ass!" Luke was immediately silent and he laid quietly until the timer went off. Then he said "Mom the timer went off." We never had a problem again. The episodes were over just like that.

Gene Therapy Trials

On the crisp sunny September morning that Luke started Kindergarten I was a mix of emotions. My little boy was starting school and he wouldn't be with me with for several hours a day. What would happen if he fell? Or the teacher wasn't there for him? I had met Luke's teacher already and thought he was a very nice teddy bear of a man. He seemed like the perfect match for Luke but even this did nothing to ease my nerves.

After dropping Luke off I went to the post office to pick up our mail. There was a letter from some organization, I think it must have been the Muscular Dystrophy Association, notifying me that Luke was eligible to enter the all new "Gene Therapy Trials." I sent in Luke's application that very same day. I felt to have this news only a year after diagnosis was a sign that a cure was close.

I shared the gene therapy news with Luke's teacher and that evening he called me and asked if it would be okay for the kindergarten class to paint pictures to sell at an Art Show to help fund Luke going to the trials. I told him that Luke hadn't been picked yet, but he insisted, saying that it didn't matter and that he wanted to do this for Luke.

A few weeks later, the little masterpieces that the students painted were put on pretty water colored white cardboard and plastic wrapped. Each painting unique, each painting for Luke. Humbled and deeply touched, this was first time I felt in awe that someone did something so incredibly wonderful for Luke in the hope that he would be saved.

We found out shortly thereafter that Luke hadn't been picked for the trials. Outwardly I resonated hope and positivity, but inwardly I was crushed. The roller coaster continued as we went on living day to day.

On a Wing and a Prayer

When the MDA approached me about having Luke as their poster child for the Alaska chapter, we jumped at the chance. I had always had a bittersweet realization that I could help other people through my personal journey with Luke and DMD.

In September of 1998, Alaska Parenting Magazine journalist Kristen Seine wrote an article about Luke and me called "On a Wing and a Prayer: A 5-Year-Old Fights a Deadly Disease." The table of contents caption read, "A mother and son fight a deadly disease with faith, hope and a positive outlook." When I saw Luke's face on the front cover all I could do was cry! This only happened to other people. Not to me. I wanted so desperately to change places with someone else. There it was again. The excruciating pain that lingers below the surface every minute of every day. An agony that never totally subsides. Luke was quoted in the article saying" I can't wait to when I can run!"

The article later won the National Parenting Publications Award. Seine said, "I'm really honored that we won a national award for this story about Luke and his mother. Meeting them had a profound impact on me because their courage and positive outlook must take incredible strength. I am glad someone else was touched by their story, too."

Good Will Ambassador

Luke served as the Muscular Dystrophy Association's Goodwill Ambassador for Alaska from 1999 until 2001. Luke loved the attention and he was pampered and given gifts at every Fill The Boot Campaign or Lock Up event that we attended. But all that attention had a huge drawback when he started to expect the same treatment at home. When I asked him one day to put up his clothes, he didn't want to and said "You can't make me. You know what I have!" I instantly replied "I of all people KNOW what you have and you will not use it as a crutch to get your way! You put your clothes away right now while you still can." I then called the MDA and told them that Luke would only be doing a few appearances until he had a better attitude. I feel that kids need to be a part of the family and help out with the household chores. I also felt Luke needed to do things for himself while he still had the ability. I have never wavered from this belief.

Long Way Home

The summer had been great with working on the farm, playing with Luke and back yard barbeques. But when October came around I hadn't been feeling well. I seemed to be tired all the time and my period was a few days late. I thought I'd go to the doctor to see if I was anemic since I had had trouble with low iron levels before.

When the doctor told me I was pregnant I looked at her in shock and disbelief. Here I was in a serious relationship but not yet married, my son had muscular dystrophy and I had a 50-50 chance of having another affected child. This was not news that I was ready to hear. Before I headed home from the doctor's office to tell Glen the news, I took the long way home in an effort to get my head on straight. I had to be absolutely sure what I was going to do no matter what Glen decided or wanted. I felt that if we were going to have a child, we were going to do it happily and on purpose knowing full well what we were up against. After all every life is miraculous!

Glen was sitting on the couch and I was sitting on the floor, crying with my back against the couch, my legs stretched out under the coffee table. I can't remember the exact words I used to tell Glen he was going to be a daddy, but I do remember how quiet he was, how unreadable he was. I remember being so worried about what was going on in his mind. I told him that I understood if having a child wasn't what he wanted but that I intended on having the baby with or without him. I said that if he chose to be with me and the baby, we would both have to agree on it happily. And of course, we talked about the possibility of having a child with Duchenne together.

Glen broke his silence by saying we were having a girl. I said, "We?" and he said, "Yes cause we were going to get married!" I said, "No we aren't, you haven't asked me yet." He jumped up and ran to the phone and called my dear friend Donna the wedding coordinator and asked her if she would go ring shopping with him. He then proceeded to make several calls, all to family, telling them, "We are pregnant and getting married!"

We decided on a January wedding because I'd be only 4 months along and not showing too much. I put my boys in matching tuxedos with tails. Glen told Luke the tails were "mud flaps." I'll never figure out boys and their fascination with car parts.

Now that I had told Glen, Luke was next. I was pretty sure he would be more than okay with having a sibling, possibly even excited. I was right. He was only 8 years old and he'd never been around anyone that was pregnant before. I don't think he really understood what was happening until I started to show. The baby would get hiccups all the time and Luke thought that was pretty cool. He would put his little hand on my tummy to feel the hiccups. He loved watching my tummy "bump up" as he called it.

On July 11, 1999, our baby girl Jenna was born two weeks early. I nearly died from a pulmonary embolism after giving birth and was in pretty bad shape but she was perfect. I called her Pumpkin, daddy called her Turnip, and Luke fondly called her Pickle. She was so cute and she completed our family. Luke immediately took on the big brother role with pride. Now Luke had a sister to love and to be loved by.

Chapter Three

Luke and Puppy Max, 1998

Luke was having a hard time walking through
the snow, especially with heavy winter boots.
He wanted so bad to be able to run with
his dog. So I put him in the sled and I would
run while pulling him so Max could run
with Luke.

I Can Heal My Life

In Chapter two I mentioned I found myself living a life I had never dreamed, with an incredible chance at a life of my choice. I never dreamed I would have to face the probable human outcome of my own child dying before me, much less finding the love of my life. Here I was madly in love with Glen and our home spun farm lifestyle while trying with all my might to focus on the positive, not my son dying. I knew I had to dig to the depths of my soul with courage to find a braveness I wasn't sure I even had.

When I was a kid, average was viewed as okay because at least that meant I was passing and not being a problem. You could say I was not taught how to be the best me or to even love myself. But I knew I had to figure it out. If for no other reason than to not be debilitated by grief I felt for Luke, not to mention I was a wife to an incredible guy and I was a mother of not just one child but two. They depend on me. A friend of mine at the time suggested I read a book titled, You Can Heal Your Life by Louise Hay. I completely resonated with the fact that the point of power is now, the present moment, and that thoughts are all we are ever dealing with at any given time, with the best part being able to change our thoughts!

The book also brought to my attention that we must nurture the body, mind and spirit as one. HMMM, you mean I could choose what I am thinking about Luke's disease and that I am not a bad person being punished after all, that I could choose to rise above to live life with courage and triumph? That I could actually love and give myself all that I need? My soul soaked up this new information like a sponge. I wanted to live like this; I wanted to raise Luke and Jenna with this knowledge, which I have, but also at the time I had this idea since my son and I had been dealt a "Bad Hand" no more bad things would ever happen again, life would run smoothly and everyone would understand. This was also the time I figured out that there are three kinds of people in this world. First kind are the angles who truly care, wanting to help and make a difference...they totally "get" you and your current situation. Second are the ones who mean well and say they understand but really don't. These are the kind that can be the most challenging and third...my favorite, which I write about with clenched teeth are the kind that really don't give a damn, the heck with you and the outcome as long as they get their job done...GRRRR!!! All issues that have come up over the years have had elements of ease and elements of great anguish and pain, with the latter two kinds of people always the crux of the matter.

Wheelbarrow

Luke went from liking school to not wanting to go. Come to find out he was having troubles in P.E. class. Luke was seven at the time. I called up the Ms. PE to see if I could find out what was going on. I asked her if she had read Luke's file. And she said she had and invited me in to one of her classes with Luke. All the kids were broken up in partners. Luke and I were paired as well. There were stations set up around the gym, we came to the wheelbarrow station. You know where one partner holds up the legs of the other so they can walk using just their arms. Luke had never been able to hold up his own weight with just his arms, so he started to cry. MS P.E. says to Luke,...Come on Luke show your mom you can do it. I have seen you do it before." My mind screamed, What! I was so frustrated and hurt. One because the P.E. teacher obviously did not understand and two Luke, my little boy did not have the strength to do the wheelbarrow and three I was not sure how to fix the problem. I waited for the teacher after school to speak with her. I was around six months pregnant and very emotional. Ms. PE looked down at my tummy and said, "I think we should talk about this when you are less emotional." Are you kidding me?? To make a long story short, I ended up putting Luke in adaptive P.E. Hence the problem was fixed.

Ms. Sped Bus

I was lying in the hospital bed after just delivering my daughter, which almost cost me my life. Luke was supposed to start summer school where he would also get his physical therapy done when I got a call from my grandmother who was watching Luke that the bus did not show up to take Luke to school. I immediately called the special ed busing department at our local school bus barn to find out why because they had picked him up the previous week from his dad's house. Ms. Sped Bus informed me that she did not feel that it was right for joint shared custody parents to make the bus come to both houses. I said, "So that is your opinion. My tax dollars help pay busing so what was the difference?" She said, Well we just can't pick him up at both houses." Had to get student support services involved in that one.

Bath Tub Fun

At the time we had a HUGE bright lipstick red bathtub...I loved to fill it up with bubbles and have crazy fun with the kids. I had gotten in the habit of taking pictures. This was right before digital cameras became the rage. I went and picked up the photos. I remember I couldn't wait to look at them. I ripped open the envelope. I flipped through the pictures. I suddenly stopped. There in the tub was my chubby little eight month old baby girl and the skinniest, sickliest bony kid stared smiling back at me. He looked like a holocaust victim. Tears sprang to my eyes and I ran all the way to the car. I vomited and sobbed. Flashing before my eyes was the death of Luke. I had this deep sense Luke wouldn't live past his 14th birthday! I called my in-home support person Gwen. She came over immediately and I had the first of two complete mental break downs since Luke's diagnosis

The Luke Sled

Glen is a builder and inventor by instinct. He can turn a picture into reality. He lives for making life easier for others. He is also very very good at surprises and keeping them secret. The sled he built for Luke to pull behind the snowmobile was no different. Luke could no longer ride in front of us when we would go snowmobiling because he was getting too tall and was losing upper body strength at such an alarming rate that he could no longer stop himself from falling forward. Glen knew that we needed a suitable and safe way for Luke to still enjoy riding with us.

One day I came home to find a sled with a roll bar, lights and seat belt that Luke could operate on his own. The paint Glen chose was perfectly fitting for life on a farm that depends on John Deere Tractors: John Deere green and yellow with an old John Deere mud flap hanging from the back. Painted on the side was the name "Luke." Even though the sled was for Luke, it was like Glen had made the sled for me. Glen had figured out early on how to touch my heart and that was through Luke. It is called love.

Give me 5 + 1

I am the oldest of two other siblings, my brother, Boone four years younger and my sister Autumn is 19 years younger. Mom was having her as I was leaving home. Then coming into the VanderWeele family brought me Glen's sister and brother and their spouses.

Over a period of six years I had been blessed with not one, but five nephews! My brother having a son first, then my sister-in-law with two boys, plus one girl, my favorite niece so far. I am still holding out for my brother and sister who is 21 for more nieces. As well as my brother-in-law with two boys.

I am completely in awe of them and thrilled that I can watch them in their cute little sports uniforms running and playing like boys should. Additionally, I feel that at least Luke can experience sports through them. As I have said, my son has always been a motor head without much interest in sports except for Nascar! He loves his cousins and appreciates that they are all healthy and don't have the stress of weakening muscles. He doesn't begrudge them for having a normal childhood. Luke and I both feel extremely honored and thankful for each and every one of them.

When Luke was diagnosed my brother was 22. I am not sure what his reaction was but over the years I know he has felt very sorry for what I am going through but has told me in his very heart felt way that I am his hero. And my beautiful "little" sister who I have been connected to since in the womb, was only nine. She has always been Luke and my number one fan. The some 19 years age difference many time has put me in the mother roll, but now that she is getting older it is more of a sister roll. She is the person who is my shoulder more times than I can count. I also know it kills her inside to have to watch Luke's body deteriorate and I know her heart goes out to me continually.

Grandma with the White Chevy Truck

"God willing and the creeks don't rise," was one of my grandmother's favorite sayings. It was her way of saying anything can happen. She always drove a four wheel drive truck and she took me hiking as a little girl and we would skinny dip in the mountain lakes. Together we would go for ice cream in our jammies at two am and she was always taking photos when you least expected it. She was my rock when I needed her and she was my number one fan and Luke's best friend until the day she passed. He fondly called her "grandma with the white Chevy truck."

She died in my arms with one last smile and a tear just for me. Although I was sad about her death, I was glad she wasn't in pain from her lung cancer any longer. Her entire memorial service was dedicated to Luke. The minister read words she wrote at her celebration of life. She wrote: "Do not be afraid when it is your time to pass over to heaven. I'll be waiting, ready to hold your hand." I can just envision her with glowing light radiating from her. She went from being my rock to being Luke's guardian angel.

Chapter Four

Santa Luke, 2002, Ms. McNiven, 3rd Grade
The progression of Duchenne starting to take its toll. Luke could still walk a bit, only used the wheelchair at school or long trips.

Freedom

If I tried hard enough I could go for days, sometimes even a couple months cruising along like everything was normal until I would drive by a soccer field or watch Luke get up from the floor, when overwhelming anguish and fear would send me downward, reeling and grieving. At these times I would go rent a sad movie, turn off the phone and grab the box of tissues and hide until I felt better.

It was a strange kind of surreal time. I had one child losing independence and another gaining it. I was ultra-sensitive to the internal tug-of-war that I felt inside between happiness and sadness. I was buying new walking shoes, ice skates and jump ropes for one child and leg braces and wheelchairs for the other. The dreaded idea of having to put Luke in a wheelchair was becoming a reality. In my mind it made Duchenne more real, more devastating. I wondered and feared what Luke would think and how family and others would react. Would kids pick on him? How would we get the wheelchair into our home? Was it time? How old were Duchenne boys normally put into a wheelchair? I remember thinking that God picked the wrong person for the job. The stress I felt was often times insurmountable. However I always ended right back to the thought that it was how I was thinking about what was happening that was causing such stress. So if I could flip my thoughts to more positive I could not feel as much pain. I would have this chat with myself, "Okay Misty, you got a choice here, stay miserable or ask to be shown the way.

Besides Glen and his family at my side, I had very little support from my immediate family. I don't think they knew how to support me and so it was easier to pretend that none of it was happening. My mom tried and would babysit the kids from time to time, but I could tell that she was having a hard time with it, especially Luke's physical decline.

Call From The School Nurse

The decision to order the wheelchair came after a horrible incident at school. I received a phone call from the school nurse saying that there had been an accident and that I should come and get Luke, who she said was OK but shaken up. She then told me that

Luke had been trampled by another class that was headed out to recess. Have you ever had one of those calls where you just can't believe what the person on the other end is saying? This was one of those kinds of calls.

I tried to keep my car under the speed limit as I shot over to the school. The sting of tears was blinding me and my heart was breaking. I bounced from feeling anger greater than I had ever felt to a burning exploding urgency that I can only describe as a primal instinct to protect my child. How could any of this be happening to my sweet boy? That day I knew it was time for a wheelchair.

When I got to school, I learned that the class that trampled Luke had a substitute teacher who was unaware of the situation. This did little to make me feel better, as I think Luke's physical weakness should be mentioned to every member of staff and anyone else working at the school. The minute I laid eyes on Luke, I knew that he was upset. I hugged him tight but said nothing as I needed to calm down.

Later that night I held him close and told him I was sorry for what had happened and I asked him what he thought about having a wheelchair to use at school. He was apprehensive but thought it would be great to try.

Blessing in Disguise

We had decided that the wheelchair would be used only at school until Luke needed it more. This would ensure that he wouldn't fall or be trampled. Although that gave some relief, it didn't change the fact that DMD was ever present in Luke's little body. Every step down the path of DMD's progression meant one step nearer to death. Still in my face, no matter what I did.

The day the wheelchair was dropped off I silently wept until I saw Luke's face. This new contraption had the one thing that Luke loved most: WHEELS! Luke's smile lit up the entire school gym. His excitement was so obvious, like a teenager over their first car. Finally Luke could feel the wind in his face as he raced down the hallway or across the parking lot. For once Luke could feel freedom and mobility for himself, all by himself. The wheelchair was a blessing in disguise and it gave Luke a huge esteem boost. You could see and feel the relief he felt to finally feel safe.

Luke took off like a pro, like he had been driving his entire life! Glen told him to keep his mouth closed as to not get bugs stuck in his teeth. Later we took Luke over to the farm to show Glen's parents. We loaded the wheelchair into the back of Glen's truck because we didn't have a van yet. Glen told his dad, Ben, how heavy the little Junior Model electric wheelchair was but Ben was having none of it. He said "Oh no, how much could that thing weigh?" and dared Luke to drive over his foot. Luke looked at him to make sure it was okay and then drove over Ben's foot. Ben never asked Luke to drive over his foot again.

A few months later we bought a minivan and suitcase ramp so we could haul Luke and his wheelchair around. Luke was still walking a bit, but it was sure nice to be able to take Luke places without worrying about him falling or getting too tired.

The wheelchair did bring one new problem. How in the heck were we to get it into our house? I contacted our in-home support person Gwen and she found a one-time Alaska Housing grant available for disability home modifications. The grant was just enough to cover the cost of building a ramp for a two story home.

Now the only problem was having a wheelchair and a crawling baby in the same house. Luke was extra careful not to run over his baby sister. Then as she began to walk she would stand and hold onto the back and Luke would give her rides. She loved it!

Cherish These Days

Instinctively I reached for both of my children, Jenna eight months, Luke almost nine, and the life I was creating with Glen. I decided to cherish each and every minute, every precious moment. I wanted to live life to the fullest and with as much purpose as I could muster. So when the phone call came in from The Make-A-Wish Foundation, an organization that grants "wishes" to children with life threatening medical conditions, I took it as a sign that I was on the right track. But that call also hit me like a big wave of reality because only kids that are going to die get "wishes." Death was yet again in my face.

Luke originally wanted to go to Hawaii, but the foundation said it would be hard to find activities for Luke to do for an entire week. His second choice was Disney World in Florida. Jenna was only eight months old so we decided that she would not go with us. What a trip it was with me and my new husband and Luke's dad and his girlfriend! It doesn't sound very traditional, but boy was it a blast for all of us! Luke took turns sleeping in each parents' room, so the couples could go out for grownup fun every other night.

By this point my relationship with Pat was calm and reserved as we had been divorced nearly six years. That's plenty of time for the waters to settle. We both want what is best for Luke and somehow we seem to push our thoughts, feelings and the past aside. I guess we were never a very good match as our personalities are completely different. Pat is quiet and hard to read while I am a spitfire full of chaotic energy. I need to have several things on the fire at once and I like decisions to be made quickly. I don't understand others who sit on the fence or don't show their feelings.

I have some sad memories of that trip too and looking back, I suppose I was a mess in the lead up to it. I had so much on my mind that when we got to Disney World, I discovered that I had left my purse on the plane with all of my money, my identification, and my cell phone in it. I never got any of it back. Even walking the streets of Disney and hearing all the music triggered a deep sense of nostalgia and heart wrenching pain. Luke's delighted smile had me wondering how many more years I would have with him. Would it kill me to lose him? What about my daughter?

I was a bit of a confused mess, trying to be fun, organized and happy for Luke while I was dying inside. I had a lot of conversations with myself about the importance of pulling it together, to bite the bullet and go on. My choices were either wallow in self-pity or grab the reins and look for the positive.

Here Comes Santa Claus

Grade school Christmas programs are every parent's delight, seeing children with their goofy little smiles and cute little bodies singing "Here Come Santa Claus" a little off key. It was Luke's second Christmas with his wheelchair and the teacher thought it would be a great idea to have Luke play Santa Claus with eight classmates as reindeer. Luke was the cutest, skinniest little kid in a red Santa suit that I had ever seen. He wore painted on red cheeks and a Santa hat, held the reins of his reindeer, and shouted " HO, HO, HO!" It was a wonderful sight through my tears of joy. Luke was included as a "normal" kid. The teacher just smiled and as I teared up; so did other parents. Everyone was clapping.

Luke's grade school years were filled with tons of support from teachers and Luke's physical therapists. There were several of us parents with "special kids" and we bonded close together. Even one of Luke's teachers had a blind son. This made for an accepting environment which I am very grateful for because middle school was an entirely different matter altogether.

Human Pancake

When Luke was 11, his three-year-old sister Jenna was a bundle of energy. Luke's wheelchair enabled him to keep up with his little sister and he would race along behind her as she ran as fast as she could. Luke would yell, "I'm gonna get you!" and the two of them would laugh and laugh.

Well, electric wheelchairs have this feature that makes them automatically stop on a dime if the driver lets up on the joystick. Luke could really gather up some speed in our big house and one day, he let off the joystick too soon and went flying face first onto the floor. SMACK! His front tooth nearly pierced the skin of his lip. As I raced to help him, my soul was screaming and all I could do was cry with him as he lay there bleeding, unable to get himself up. That was the day that Luke started wearing a seatbelt.

Shiny Penny

The Muscular Dystrophy Association provides a yearly "Summer Camp" where kids with MD can go for a week and feel like normal kids that fit in with everyone else. For Luke, camp has always been a highlight of the summer. The year that stands out most in my mind is the year that I brought my mother-in-law with me to drop off Luke.

I have always gone with a more holistic approach to Luke's healthcare and I am proud of the level of care that he receives. Every summer he spends many many hours outside in the sun and by August, he sports a pretty good tan. If it weren't for his wheelchair, he would look like a vision of good health. He doesn't take regular medications and he looks like any other teen, complete with a touch of acne. When we went over to the nurse's station to drop off Luke's liquid vitamins and Probiotics, I noticed the HUGE pile of medicines dropped off by other parents for their kids. I wondered just how many of those medications were truly necessary? I looked around and saw so many overweight kids with sickly faces that I almost felt guilty that Luke was so healthy. As we drove away I glanced over at my mother-in-law and saw tears in her eyes. She said, "Luke looks so good. I said, "I know, he looks like a shiny penny compared to those other kids." We just cried together. She then told me that I was doing a great job with him.

Alaskan Outdoor Fun

While MDA summer camp is the highlight of Luke's summer, what we do every March is the highlight of the winter. We pack up everything we own, put the snowmobiles, sleds and gear on a trailer and head north up the Parks Highway to the Cottini's Larson Lake Lodge about 100 miles away. Bonnie and Pio schedule a weekend every winter just for Luke to come out and ice fish, visit and "kick it" out on the deck. They always provide a memorable time, from fireworks to the outdoor hot tub to watching the stars at night.

Oh, and did I mention that the cabins don't have running water or electricity and there's no road to get there? The only way you can get there in the winter is by snowmobile, dog sled or airplane. A few can make it by cross country skiing or mountain biking, but that's clearly not an option for a family that includes a wheelchair. For us, going by snowmobile is by far the easiest way. But easy is a relative term when you consider that we have to take Luke's 500 pound power wheelchair, his manual wheelchair, his bed, and his bi-pap and cough assist machines out there.

Once there we have to take care of Luke's needs, like going to the bathroom, cold weather protection and sleeping. Over the years we have put our minds to the task and have come up with some pretty cool ideas to make it all happen and give Luke a family fun winter vacation.

For me, going to 'the cabin' as we call it, puts Luke's progression of Duchenne right up close in my face with nowhere to run. At home, modern conveniences and my daily routines make things easier and take my mind off the fact that DMD is ravaging Luke's body at a very sickening and alarming rate. But at the cabin, it is all so "In Your Face!" It's hard enough taking care of him at home, but doing it in a place where there is no indoor plumbing or electricity takes it to a whole new level for everyone in the family. Emotionally it is always a challenge and one year, I had my second DMD induced mental breakdown. I locked myself in the bathroom and cried like I have never cried before, overwhelmed with agony and joy at the same time.

There are times when I feel like I'm the wrong person for this job. That the pain is just too much. Then something or someone comes along and reminds me it is so much easier to be happy. It always strikes me how humbled I feel for having friends like the Cottini's wanting to give Luke and our family some winter fun. Everyone needs friends like them.

Close Call

It was fall and the leaves were turning a little bit yellow and orange. The sun was out sparkling through the trees. The day was beautiful and good. I was a chaperone for a group of third graders on a school field trip based on lessons about salmon and their migration from the ocean to Alaska's streams, creeks, lakes and rivers. The Department of Fish and Game were stocking salmon in a nearby local lake and around the lake is a smooth enough trail for Luke to drive his wheelchair. At one end of the lake the water is so deep that you can't see the bottom. The section of trail around this end has a steep wooded embankment on one side. Luke was about 10 feet in front of me when I turned around to check on the other kids. As I turned, I saw Luke's wheelchair out of the corner of my eye. It was lurching forward and headed straight down the embankment toward the lake! As I took off after him, I focused on keeping his limbs from being mangled as the wheelchair flipped over and slid downward. I put everything I had into stopping the wheelchair and unclipping Luke's seatbelt, for I knew that if he went in, he would be trapped underwater. Somehow I was able to get to him before he went in. It was as if some big helping hand came down and all 350 pounds of boy and wheelchair came to a halt about half way down the embankment.

Neither one of us had a scratch on us, which was a miracle in itself because I was wearing shorts. Two dads who were also chaperoning came running and they were able to bring Luke and his wheelchair up to the trail. Later the kids told me that I literally flew down the hill after Luke like I had wings or something. The next day my entire body hurt like I had been hit by a Mack truck. Luke told me on the way home that day that he felt grandma was there. I told him that his guardian angel is always with him and that she was doing a pretty darn good job! Luke agreed.

Fifth Grade Field Trip

In celebration and farewell to Middle School every year the 5th graders head down to Homer, a small Alaska Coastal City located on Kachemak Bay, for adventure, "tide pooling" and learning about Alaskan sea life. The kids look forward to this three day field trip all winter.

Luke's teacher, Mr. Lytle, had made the trip the year before with Luke's friend Steven, who had Duchenne as well. It was decided that another parent, a father whose boy Tommy, is blind, and would go along on the trip since our boys needed extra help. Tommy's dad would be better at helping with Luke's physical needs and so we thought it would work better if he acted as Luke's legs and I acted as

Tommy's eyes. I was happy with this because you can imagine how hard it is to push a manual wheelchair through sand and rocks. Our arrangement worked out very well and was extra special since Luke and Tommy were good friends.

This trip was a challenge for me. I usually keep myself busy by focusing on Luke's needs and my daily routine but now I watched someone else do everything that needs doing for my boy. I forced myself to stay focused because I had to help Tommy navigate the beach terrain but I couldn't help but worry about all of the physical work that Tommy's dad was doing for Luke. There were many times when Luke's teacher would grab the front of the wheelchair and Tommy's dad would grab the back and they could carry Luke down the beach to all of the action happening at the tide pools. I felt torn. On one hand, what an incredible sight to have two grown men helping and caring for Luke and on the other hand, there was Duchenne glaring at me.

Luke was also taking his own frustration about his lack of mobility out on me. I am sure that being a pre-teen didn't help matters much. During dinners back at the school where we were staying, Luke would sit with his friends and tell me to sit somewhere else even though he needed my help to eat. Luke had never treated me like this before. All I wanted to do was run and hide. I was embarrassed that Luke was treating me this way but at the same time, I was devastated that Luke required so much assistance. It was apparent that Luke didn't like it either.

Chapter Five

Jenna, Misty, Glen and Luke Before Back Surgery, 2005

Luke was so used to his body he didn't realize how slumped over and uncomfortable
he was or even that his feet were curling in from lack of use and muscle deterioration.

Every Life is Precious

By this stage of the journey, despite the consuming pain of watching Luke deteriorate physically, the beauty that shows through in life, like the flower growing between the cracks of the sidewalk or the mother holding hands with her child as they cross the road, was all around me and ever present. I just had to look. You see every life is precious from the moment of conception to the day we die. No one knows when it's their time to pass. It could be today, it could be tomorrow, but we will all pass over. It is a guarantee.

But sometimes it did feel like time was moving too quickly. Luke was walking less and less and I worried about how I was going to be able to take care of him. I felt very strongly that it wasn't Luke's stepdad's ultimate responsibility to provide what Luke needed. I really didn't know what I was doing but with the help of my in-home support person, Gwen, I literally went on a mission to find out what I needed to do to provide for Luke's increasing needs. I found several grants for medical equipment and modifying our bath room and our 80 foot of ramp so Luke could get into the house. I also jumped right in to special needs workshops, learning everything I needed to know about advocating, day to day care and the school system.

Time went on and I was able to get everything that Luke needed and at the same time start my own business. Looking back I see that I was keeping myself extra busy with life so the pain didn't seem so real. That just maybe there would either be a cure or Luke would pass so the madness would end.

Middle school is often a tough time for any pre-teen but even more so for a middle school boy in a wheelchair. Luke was bored and we were having trouble with his behavior. He would lash out at his aides, his teachers, and even at me. Luke later shared with me that he felt like he was cursed and that he was very frustrated with life at the time. He remembers one teacher telling his aide to go to the office while she locked the door and put Luke's wheelchair in manual mode so he couldn't go anywhere. That's the equivalent of holding someone down and not letting them get up. We fondly call this teacher "Fairy Godmother from Shrek 2": the hair, the glasses, the sweet and nice person on the outside hiding the mean and unhappy person on the inside.

Those three years of middle school were full of dreadful, hard times that attacked me and challenged me on every level. Physically, Luke was getting bigger and it was hard on me to always be picking him up. Mentally it seemed a challenge with every teacher. Duchenne Muscular Dystrophy was ravaging my boy's body with a vengeance: he was starting to slump over from scoliosis and that in turn put pressure on his bowels, lungs and internal organs. I wondered when it was going to end and spiritually, I was beginning to wonder about the real meaning of life. We were being forced to make hard and life-altering medical decisions which would impact Luke and the entire family for the rest of our lives. I also worried that Luke's dad might be a challenge as it was evident that he was having a hard time accepting Luke's Duchenne. I also had to consider the emotional wellbeing of my daughter who was starting to worry about her brother.

Brother and Sister

There are nearly eight years between Luke and Jenna so it wouldn't seem that they would be close but this isn't the case. Sure, they have their sibling quarrels and are sometimes jealous of each other but their bond has always been strong. From the day that Jenna was born, Luke has been very much the overprotective big brother. I took him with us when Jenna needed shots as a baby and when she would cry, Luke would be furious at the nurse for hurting her. As Jenna has gotten older her protectiveness and awareness of Luke and his medical condition have only proven to strengthen their relationship.

When Luke started using his wheelchair and could no longer get up from the floor, Glen bought a pre-made laminate countertop and put legs on it, making it the perfect height for Luke and his wheelchair. Jenna sits on a bar stool on one side and Luke on the other and this small invention has enabled them to play with each other. During the early years, the play was pretty much all imaginary and board games.

Now the "Big Table" is Lego Nation and is used mostly for building things. Luke and Jenna have figured out how to satisfy the 10-year-old engineer in Jenna while promoting Luke's ingenuity. And let's face it, at 18 Luke has little interest in pretend play.

Another one of my favorite things to watch is when they tie a wagon to Luke's wheelchair in the summer or a sled in the winter and he pulls Jenna around. She screams and throws her hands up in a gesture like it is the fastest ride she has ever been on!

Hand Bell Hell

Remember when I told you that there are three kinds of people in this world and that the people who say they understand but really don't can cause the most frustration? Well this is what Luke being in the hand bell choir was like. Luke could still hold the light hand bells and play small segments of the music and his teacher, Mr. Music, said he was working out a way for Luke to continue to play. Although he may have tried, in the end Mr. Music could not put his desire for perfection aside in order to help give Luke some much needed self-esteem. He insisted that Luke play music that was much too hard for him physically and then he vented his frustration out at him. I simply could not understand this man's reasoning and attitude and when the situation became untenable, I felt I had no choice but to take Luke out of the class. It was a hard lesson for me because I have always believed that you have to follow through with your commitments and Luke had made a commitment to the hand bell choir. But DMD makes you change many of your long held beliefs and this was just another example of that.

Stephanie

The phone call came in the morning on the day after the Fourth of July. My friend Tesa's 19-year-old daughter Stephanie had been killed in a freak car accident. I rushed to the funeral home to meet Tesa and her husband. I sat with her when the funeral director told her it would not be a good idea for her to see her daughter's body. I watched her pick out the urn and make all the funeral arrangements. My heart ached for her. About a year later while talking on the phone, Tesa told me she didn't know how I did it. She said what I was going through with Luke was harder than losing her Stephanie. I said "No Way! At least I still have Luke with me." I was shocked that she considered my pain worse! Isn't pain pain? She has to live each day without ever seeing her daughter again, and I have to live each day waiting for the other shoe to drop while watching muscle weakness take over Luke's body. But Luke is still very much alive and I cherish each day with him.

Before Stephanie's death I had always thought that losing a child would kill you. I couldn't see how a parent could go on. Watching Tesa and her family go on has been enlightening. They have proven to me that life goes on. That you can treasure this life and the many gifts and little miracles that make it worth living. Life is meant to be lived full on!

Lesson in Water Safety

My aunt had a big family party to celebrate the July 4th holiday at her lake house. All of us were having a ball barbecuing, swimming and jet skiing. Luke was 11 and was already on his second wheelchair after growing out of the first cute little junior model. He drove down to the water's edge where my brother was about to take three or four little cousins out for a ride on the jet ski and so we put Luke in a life jacket a little too big for him, tied it tight and put him on the jet ski in the front of my brother. They made several trips back and forth in front of the beach. Things got a little rowdy out there with all of the kids tipping the thing from side to side. It went over a little bit too far and it turned onto its side, throwing everyone into the water. Luke and my brother landed on the side facing away from the beach so we could not see what was going on. My brother frantically yelled, "HELP!" and my cousin tore off his shirt and dove in to assist. A couple of others grabbed the canoe. I stood there not at all worried at first, until it dawned on me that my brother was having a hard time keeping both himself and Luke above water. I waited silently. I felt if I moved something worse would happen.

They came ashore and my brother told me he was sorry and I hugged him. He then told us what had happened: My brother was wearing blue jeans and they got so heavy when he went into the water that he could barely swim. Then Luke slipped through his life jacket! These two factors almost cost someone's life! A very big lesson. A) always wear a life jacket and B) always wear a life jacket.

After the lake incident my brother seemed unsure of how to handle Luke. I think it scared him so much that he now keeps his distance. I know he loves Luke and me dearly but that was just too close of a call for him.

Secret Christmas Project

"The Greatest Stepdad on Earth" is what Luke calls Glen. One of Glen's gifts is a natural talent for making things and he can fix anything almost blindfolded. He takes great pride in being able to make life easier for Luke and he has enabled Luke to have life experiences that would not have been possible without his resourcefulness and ingenuity. Needless to say, all of this makes me love him that much more.

During one Christmas season, my sister Autumn, who was 15 at the time, was living with us and doing a secret project with Glen. On many occasions she would show up with red paint on her clothes wearing a big smile. Glen would just walk by smiling that smile that says he has a secret and he isn't going to share it.

On Christmas morning Glen got up and said he would be right back. Pretty soon thereafter I heard a noise like a tractor engine and looked out the window. Sure enough there appeared a John Deere Tractor pulling a red Santa sleigh complete with Christmas lights. I thought we would just have to lift Luke and sit him up front in the seat, but no, Glen had made the sleigh with Luke AND his wheelchair in mind. It had a drop down ramp out the back so Luke could drive right up into it. I still get misty-eyed remembering that Christmas.

All of The Above

I hear many parents say Duchenne wasn't in their plans. My response is that I didn't have a plan. Fourteen years ago I was a going nowhere fast single mom who knew that her life wasn't working but had absolutely no idea how to change it. Then the Duchenne explosion happened and my world changed beyond anything I could have dreamed. Fate led me down a path that has enabled me to live a life that I would not have thought possible.

Glen and I met each other in the good old fashion way: at a bar. He would ask me to dance and I would say no. I had convinced myself that he was not my type because he looked too young and tried too hard. Once, after turning him down, he left and quickly returned with a rose that he had made out of a paper napkin. I had to dance with him then! It was the sweetest gesture that I had ever seen and it sure beat the usual pickup lines. He was a surprisingly great dancer and he liked to talk to me but I still didn't take him seriously for almost two years. I would show up at the bar and he would make a beeline over to me with a paper rose in hand. It was a bit annoying but we would usually spend the evening dancing to every song. Slowly, I began to realize that I missed him on those nights that he didn't show up.

My relationship with Glen took a turn on the day that Luke was diagnosed. My cousin Kelley had driven my ex-husband Pat and me to the hospital where we heard the news. After we dropped the boys off at Pat's house, Kelley turned to me and asked, "Now what." I said, "Take me to the farm, " and she said, "That's the best damn news I have heard all day."

Up until this point Glen and I had just started dating a bit, but I was taking it very slow and he didn't seem to mind that. He didn't expect anything from me. He seemed to like Luke and the farm where he lived was spectacular. As I mentioned earlier, I was born in the farm's driveway and this made me feel connected to the place. When Kelly and I pulled into the driveway that day, there was Glen in a stark white t-shirt walking up to the house with the sunshine on his back. I ran up to him and he stood there holding me, while I cried my soul out explaining to him what had just happened.

When we drove away I remember thinking that I had most likely just lost him. I suddenly became a lot to take on for a man who was still living at home and had never been married. I thought that being with Luke and me was a guaranteed heartache now, so I was a little taken aback when he called me a week later to see if I needed anything. In my grief, I blurted out that Luke wanted a kitty. Glen brought two. Luke named them Alley Cat and Scaredy Cat.

During those first months post-diagnosis, any time I felt that I was going to die from the pain, Glen would pick me up on his motorcycle and we would ride. On the farm I would walk the fields breathing in the scenery and ride beside him in the tractor. Our relationship began to take on a life of its own. We'd get close and then I would back away. I broke up with Glen several times before I finally figured out that he offered me something that I had never had. Normal. I asked him to bear with me and I am sure glad that he did.

I started calling Glen "All Of The Above" shortly after I realized that I loved him. He fills the broken pieces in my heart. Being with Glen has taught me to love myself.

Chapter Six

Luke and Jenna, 2008

This picture says it all. They look so very proud of each other. The love they share is evident.

All About Luke

As Luke's 14th birthday approached, my insides were all bunched up waiting for the other shoe to drop. I started catching myself holding my breath during the day. I was angered easily and was running on nothing but emotion, most of it anger and sadness. Even taking care of Luke's daily needs started to annoy me, which brought on an enormous feeling of guilt. I wanted to be Luke's rock, not an overbearing mother who took her anger and annoyance out on her children. I knew I needed to do something instead of waiting for Luke to die. This wasn't a way to live. And it definitely wasn't fun.

Middle school hell was over for Luke and he was now in high school. Luke enjoyed school more now, but for me, high school brought me a bag full of brand new fears. The high school had more students and thus more commotion, fighting, cliques, etc. How was Luke going to avoid getting hurt physically and emotionally? How could he defend himself? What if he had a medical emergency and no one would help him?

Luke was also going into his freshman year right after his back surgery. We chose the end of the summer, one week before school started, for the surgery so that Luke could enjoy being outside all summer. Even though the timing made things a bit tricky, I felt like I could handle the red tape at school because I was pretty experienced in all things Duchenne by this stage of the game. I had dealt with my son's diagnosis, I had watched him lose his ability to walk, I'd handled a ton of school complications and misunderstandings, not to mention busing issues, in home care issues, and dual household issues.

Before high school started for Luke, I wanted to make sure I hadn't missed anything about going into this new situation and so I called a meeting with Luke's entire new team. Luke needed a male aide to assist him with his school day and he needed an entirely new IEP because his old one was crap! I wanted to take a peek at the new landscape that Luke would be in for the next four years.

Luke's New Hero

Luke and I were crammed into a room with a table much too large for the space. One by one Luke's new team came in and introduced themselves. Then this guy with a twinkle in his eye that I could see even through his glasses smiled at me and said, "Mom, this isn't about you, this is all about Luke, I hope you don't mind." I was relieved and thought "FINALLY someone who gets this whole thing!" The meeting proceeded without any interruption from me. For the first time, "Mr. School" was talking to Luke and wanting to know what he wanted to get out of high school, his life and his future.

For Luke it was very liberating. After years spent in special education, Luke wanted and needed more. Later, after the meeting, Luke said, "I think I am going to like it here. They actually talk to me! I feel like they care."

Later, when Luke met with Mr. School to go over his old Individual Education Plan (IEP), Mr. School read a few things in it and then chucked the entire plan into the garbage can right in front of Luke! He said Luke was smart and didn't need to be in special ed. That day they made a plan to prepare Luke for general education: a plan that would give Luke the tools to advocate for himself. Just in case you don't know, an IEP is a customized educational plan for children with special needs. It gives teachers and school administrators a written guide about the supports such a student needs to receive an equal opportunity education. If it isn't written in the IEP, the school legally doesn't have to do jack for a special needs child. All too often, school districts employ some teachers and staff who don't want to deal with special needs students. The IEP is designed to protect such students and give them the support they need to succeed.

Social Isolation

The social isolation of boys with Duchenne is not intentional but it's a very hard thing to cope with as a parent. I can't put my finger on exactly when it started to happen. It's more like something that slowly creeps into your life that you don't notice until it suddenly slaps you in the face. It's not like other kids aren't nice to Luke; it's just that their activities usually involve physical feats that just aren't possible for him.

When Luke was in middle school, I learned of another boy who lived locally with another type of muscular dystrophy. This boy, Cody, had met Luke at MDA Summer Camp and so Cody's mother and I decided to get the two together. Cody's disease requires a ton of medical equipment and so Luke always went to his house. He stayed all night on a couple of occasions, but then Cody's condition worsened, which in turn scared Luke enough to stop going.

As I said, the social isolation is heartbreaking as a parent. Although Luke seems to handle it very well. I know it bothers him to not be included with his peers. We focus on family and Luke has his younger siblings to play with. As a family, we try to keep him busy and include him in as many events we possible. The fact that Luke has two families also helps with the boredom and sort of picks up the slack of not having peers to hang out with.

Luke is constantly surrounded by adults and he is comfortable with that. He has become the master of his own destiny and he gets involved with things of his own choosing, like high school dances. He is learning to say hi and pick up conversations with other students. From talking with other young men living with Duchenne, I gather that college is much better. Luke can't wait.

Down To The Bone

Luke had already been using his wheelchair for a few years full time as his muscles weakened and he lost strength, which is sadly the normal progression of Duchenne. He started favoring one side of his body more and his spine began to curve over, causing scoliosis. He was also becoming incontinent and having aches and pain he hadn't had before. Over time if his back went untreated, Luke's left lung would most likely collapse. This meant one thing and one thing only.

It was time to consider a surgical procedure called spinal fusion where they insert and tie together two titanium rods down both sides of the spine.

Luke's father and I did a lot of research about the surgery and what would likely happen if we opted not to do it. We both felt that there really was no other option. The idea that these were our two options sickened me further and backed me into a corner, ripping my heart and mind right in two. I had always felt that I would instinctively know when it was Luke's time to pass, but when I had to decide whether to go ahead with Luke's full spinal fusion surgery, my insecurities bombarded me and I wavered. So many questions loomed before me and I wondered if I had done everything possible for my boy. "Would I lose my baby during surgery? Did we wait too long? What is life going to be like after the surgery? Will he still be able to feed himself?" Any surgery is very risky for a DMD boy because of complications that can arise from the use of anesthesia.

These questions kept plaguing me and I often woke up sweaty and scared out of my mind. As I mentioned earlier, I had a premonition years before that Luke would not live past the age of 14 and at the time of the surgery, he was not quite 15!

Another thing making me crazy about the surgery was the timing of it. At the end of the summer, harvest in Alaska is in full swing and that meant that I would be facing Luke's surgery without Glen, my number one support person. I was absolutely terrified!

Once Luke went into surgery, the agony of waiting was excruciating and I was an emotional wreck. I sat waiting with my mom, my sister and my aunt. Luke's dad, Pat, and his new girlfriend, Bessie, sat in a windowed nook some distance away. Every so often Pat would walk past me to the bathroom with a sick look on his face. The stress heightened when I looked up to find several of my family members all walk in at the same time looking like they had lost their best friend. My heart dropped. "Did they know something I didn't?"

I found out soon enough that my family had just received news that a cousin had gone over a ravine in his car and was found two days later, alive but in need of surgery. Ironically, he had been helicoptered to the same hospital and was waiting on Luke's operating room!

In all, Luke's surgery was nine hours long. He spent a total of eight days in the hospital and he only needed eight weeks of bed rest at home before returning back to school instead of the standard 12 weeks normally required for recovery from such surgery. He healed very quickly. In recovery I unexpectedly witnessed love in its truest form. The doctor had just removed the breathing tube from Luke's lungs and Luke was sort of freaking out. My ex-husband's girlfriend Bessie started rubbing Luke's hand with tears streaming down her face. My heart overflowed with amazement and joy at seeing another women, another mom, love my boy entirely! I was and still am delighted that Pat found a keeper.

During Luke's recovery at home I was opening a can when the sharp metal circle came up and cut my finger. I actually heard it nick the bone! I was jumping around the kitchen holding my finger and screaming. "I cut my finger, I cut my finger all the way down to the bone!" Luke said, "That is nothing, I'll show you down to the bone!" So true! Luke's scar starts at his neck and runs all the way down to his tail bone where the rods were placed on both sides of his spine and screwed into his hip bones. When I first saw the stitches I thought I was going to pass out! Another piece of my heart broken. How was that possible? I didn't think I had anything left in there to break!

With Luke resting peacefully, I went to take a shower in the "family" shower at the hospital when I completely broke down, in shock from the horror of what my boy had just endured! What I had allowed to happen to him! But without the surgery, Luke would have been bedridden from pain and he would have had great difficulty breathing. If we had not straightened it, his spine would have slowly crushed his organs and lungs. It's a decision that no mother should ever have to make!

Run For Our Sons

When I first heard of this fundraising event by Parent Project Muscular Dystrophy, the title alone enticed me to enter the January, 2006, Disney World Marathon in Orlando, Florida. What an empowering feeling to join in a cause to help someone else, especially your very own child. And even more so when you see others joining in for your cause.

However, running a marathon meant training and training in Alaska meant winter training, which I had never done, let alone ever running an entire marathon. But I threw caution to the wind and decided to commit to run a half marathon, 13.1 miles. I got right to work and set up my First Giving fundraising page and friends started jumping in with donations. As far as training, every morning off I'd go. I hated it, but I persevered by thinking that I was doing something for Luke that he could not do himself. It also was better than sitting around watching Luke's body deteriorate.

It was very neat to be a part of something bigger. For the first time I didn't feel so alone. I felt someone finally understood. On the night before marathon day, the temperature dropped down in the low 30's. I wasn't prepared for cold at all. You'd think coming from Alaska I would have known better, but I was in the land of Florida orange juice and I was expecting warm sunshine! I have never been so cold in my life!

Nothing prepared me for the feeling of amazement that I got when I stepped off the bus at the start line. I could feel the energy in the air. I arrived early because I had no idea what to expect. There I was, this country bumpkin of a girl born and raised in a small Alaskan town and suddenly I was literally engulfed by thousands of people! UNBELIEVABLE!

And then we were off. What a feeling! I ran the first part of my race with tears streaming down my face. As daylight hit, I came around a turn and looked back at the runners all around me. I was awestruck. Suddenly I felt very small and life seemed so big, so real. Would our efforts be enough to find a cure in my son's life time? Or what about my future grandchildren?

All of these thoughts came and went, then up ahead was Cinderella's castle. But instead of feeling like a princess I felt sharp stomach pains and they didn't feel like the normal cramps that you get from running. When I finally got to a bathroom stop, I discovered the culprit: My monthly friend came in the middle of the marathon! I wasn't prepared for that. I didn't have any money on me to purchase what I needed. I was, as the saying goes, up a creek without a paddle! There I sat on the toilet crying...I had to finish, I was so close. What was I going to do? I folded toilet paper and decided to walk the rest of the way.

At 11 miles my legs were on fire, screaming at me in pain. At 12 miles I was ready to throw in the towel as I kept worrying that I was making a mess that other people could notice. Down to the last .1 of a mile, which at the time felt like another 10! I could no longer feel my legs at all. Just then I heard the crowd roar and I knew the finish line was close. I started my hobbling attempt to run across the finish line with arms outstretched. I did it! I felt accomplishment and bewilderment at the same time. I received my Donald Duck Medal and it is proudly displayed on Luke's wall next to his Dale Earnhardt Jr. poster.

Possibilities

On the Duchenne front I was meeting grown men living well into their 20s and even 30s. For the first time I realized that I was living in the box that the DMD diagnosis tries to put over your life. The "truths" that I had always believed about Luke's future were falling apart. Ideas like: There is no cure, Luke won't live past age 14, he will never have children or a mate to love him. Those parameters are so limiting! Life can be so strange and full of mystery.

As I was awakening and looking back over the last several years, it seemed like every time I hit a block or a hard point, life opened up with what I needed right at the very moment that I needed it. I slowly was beginning to realize that Luke was going to live much longer than 14 years. It was apparent that I needed to prepare myself and Luke for a future, hopefully a long one. I submitted my application to The Partners in Policy Making (PIP) Internship program. For the last 20 years PIP has been teaching parents and self-advocates the power of advocacy to change the world's perception of people living with disabilities. To change the way they are supported, viewed and taught. Taking the course was a major mental shift for me. Instead of waiting for Luke to die, I was suddenly preparing for his future. The course was so good for me. Not only did it teach me about the vast opportunities for Luke, it also opened my eyes to ways that I could fulfill my yearning to help other people.

Buggy Time

The winter before Mother's Day of 2006, Glen was locked away after work in his shop working tirelessly on a project that would get Luke from the yard to the mountains and surrounding mud holes. The best of Alaska is seen off the beaten trail and just because Luke was in a wheelchair, that wasn't going to stop Glen from figuring out another way for us all to build memories. With Luke, the favorite memories usually involve wheels, mud and family.

That was how "Luke's Buggy" was born. Using an old garbage truck that had been given to us, Glen built a flat deck with a driver's seat, back seat for the girls and wheelchair lift that he found in someone's junk pile.

Luke has gone where few have ever traveled before because of the buggy. My dream of the Alaska outdoor lifestyle for Luke is a reality and I have Glen to thank. During the summer if we aren't farming or hanging out on the deck, we are on Luke's buggy. We pack up the cooler, throw in the rubber tote that I fill with coats, blankets, toilet paper, bug spray, survival food and anything else I can think of 'just in case' and head for the river or up to the Jones's Ville Coal Mine Road to go find some scenery and hopefully some MUD!

The buggy has been featured in the National MDA Quest magazine in an article titled "Born To Be Wild." It's also on the MDA website.

Another Surgery

The muscle loss in Luke's body combined with the fact that he sits in his wheelchair pretty much all day made Luke's body start to curl inward. The back surgery fixed his back but his feet were turning inward and upward too. Shoes began to really bother him and he didn't like the way his feet began to look. So we decided to go in for heel cord lengthening surgery, figuring it would be a piece of cake compared to his nine hour back surgery.

The surgery was only about an hour from start to finish, but the aftermath was horrendous. Luke was in such severe pain after the surgery and the pain medication didn't seem to help at all. He lay there crying while everyone around him tried to make him comfortable. It was horrible for me to watch and hear my child lying there in pain that I could do nothing to change. I felt so powerless and the mother bear in me came out with a vengeance. Those poor nurses.

Steven

Luke first met Steven at school, then again at MDA Summer Camp, and from time to time we would run into him and his family at the MDA Clinic and other MDA functions like the Jerry Lewis Labor Day Telethon.

We had just seen Steven at clinic a couple of weeks before when the call came in that Steven had died. I was driving down the road and it was pouring down rain. I closed my cell phone and pulled over and sobbed for Steven's mother and the loss that she must feel. I cried for the relief I felt that it wasn't Luke. I cried for Steven. I screamed out, "NO MORE BOYS!"

A few days later at the funeral I watched Steve's brother and family carry in his casket. It was dark gray with Steve's baseball hats on top. I couldn't help but think that could be Luke. I reached for Luke's hand for a squeeze to reassure myself Luke was okay. During the service, the minister said it saddened him to think that the spot where Steven parked his wheelchair every Sunday would be empty, that today would have been the first time. The minister went on to say that when he entered the church, low and behold, another young man has honored his spot. There were two spots for wheelchairs to park next to the pews in the Church. Luke just so happened to pick the place where Steven had parked his. I lost it then, tears streamed down my face along with my mascara. Steve's death hit too close to home.

Later, as we were driving away, Luke told me he sort of wished he hadn't gone. He said it was a lot harder than he had imagined. I told him I was sorry and that I really hadn't known what to expect since we weren't that close and hardly knew Steven and his family.

Sweet 16

As Luke approached his 16th birthday, I felt so thankful that he was still with us and that he was happy and enjoying his life. I got together with Bessie and we planned a Nascar Mexican Surprise Birthday Party for Luke. We rented a local community hall big enough to hold both of his entire families and we brought in all of his favorite people, foods, and activities. For me, the best part of the whole experience was being able to plan it with such an awesome stepmom. Bessie makes sure that Luke is being taken care of like he is her own son. I love having her around and our situation works very well for Luke, which we both agree is the most important thing in the world.

To Give up or FIGHT, that is the question

When it comes to medical treatments and interventions related to the progression of Duchenne, Luke always resists and can be very stubborn. Sometimes it is like pulling teeth to get Luke to agree about what should be done. I have always felt that Luke should make his own decisions when it comes to his body. I try to lay out the facts and show him my research results, tell him my opinion and go from there. When Dr. Lungs suggested it was time for night time breathing assistance, Luke immediately put up a wall. I was so frustrated because I knew he needed help and that it would improve how he was feeling, but I could not get him to make a decision. I ordered the bi-pap anyway and started to think about how I could make it seem like a good option to Luke.

The situation suddenly became much more urgent when a few days later, I picked Luke up from school after he had spent several days at his dad's house. I saw him and was struck by how horrible he looked! As his mom, I knew something was up. We were on our way to an ear appointment and since we were already at the hospital, I decided to take him to the emergency room to see what was going on. Luke had a fit and fought me the entire time, telling me that he was fine, just a little sick.

It turned out that "a little sick" was full blown pneumonia with fever, cough, and the works. I was worried sick but still had to drop Luke back off at his dad's because it wasn't my week to have him. Once he arrived back at my house a few days later, I told him that he had to try the bi-pap for one hour a night. I told him that I would stay with him until he could tolerate it. He told me that he wasn't going to do it and I responded by saying that I would sleep on the floor of his room if I had to. He still refused to do it and I went to my room exasperated. A few minutes later I stormed back into Luke's room and had "the talk."

I know this usually means telling your teenager about sex but with a Duchenne teenager, it sometimes means "the talk" of life and death. I said, "Remember you told me you were going to fight? Well, what's it gonna be? Are you going to fight or give up?" There was a long pause before he yelled, "I'm gonna fight damn it"! Then we just cried together. He decided that the bipap wasn't so bad after all. He actually loves it now. When he first puts in on at night, his eyes roll back, he takes several large breaths and says, "Ahhh, this feels so good."

Jenna Benna

During my nine months of pregnancy with Jenna, I spent lots of time thinking about what I wanted for her. I tried very hard not to have dreams about sugar and spice and everything little girls are made of. I knew from my experience with Luke that sometimes life has different ideas.

But one of the things I did know was that I didn't expect Jenna to take care of Luke. I wanted her to have her own identity, free of any obligations other than the normal responsibilities that go with being a member of a family. Of course, Glen and I realized that Jenna would have challenges in her life because of the situation with Luke. That's why we have always tried to provide her with a strong support network of family and good friends. She is very close to her grandparents, including adopted grandmother Elinor, her aunts and uncles and her cousins.

As a baby, she was an exuberant bundle of joy and determination and she has transformed into a young girl who is sensitive, fun, smart, witty and compassionate. I never sugar coated Luke's diagnosis but looking back, I see that it might have been wise to shelter her a bit from the truth when she was very young. When she was in first and second grade, Jenna began to realize that Luke might die. She started sleeping in Luke's bed when he was away at his dad's house and her grades suffered terribly. She also whined a lot and I believe the emotions running through her were just too much to bear.

During one heart-to-heart conversation, Jenna told me that she was scared that Luke would die without her, that he would leave without saying goodbye, that she wouldn't know. I held her close and told her she would be one of the very first to hear when it was Luke's time to pass. My heart was squeezed so tight in my chest from keeping back the tears because Jenna needed me to be strong for her. She needed to feel comfort.

We held her back in second grade in order to give her more time to mature emotionally and I stopped taking her to Luke's doctor appointments. Glen and I also started spending more time with just her. Glen takes her to school in the morning for quality dad time and Jenna and I paint our toes, go hiking or go shopping together all the time. As a family we watch movies and play games together and in the summertime, we are always outside on our buggy or walking the vegetable fields.

Jenna's love for her brother is evident and she does help out with Luke, but it's by choice and not obligation. As Duchenne has taken over Luke's body, their play has changed and adapted. She does the physical stuff like putting the Legos together while Luke supervises and comes up with new and innovative ideas. They spend hours talking and she loves to watch Luke play his video games.

As for me, I love having a daughter who is all giggles and pinkness, who cares deeply about matching outfits and shoes. Our talks about our hopes and dreams are different and I am so thankful that she can turn to me when she needs me. It is also an incredible experience to not worry about her health, although the fact that she might be a carrier of Duchenne is of concern to me. One day, she can find out her status and decide on her own future with regard to children. I did not have a choice and I want it to be different for my daughter. What can I say, she is my girl.

You Might Be a Red Neck If

Luke loves anything with Jeff Foxworthy, Larry the Cable Guy and the Here's Your Sign guy, Bill Engvall. Luke even went through a time writing his own red neck stories. He loves pretty much anything redneck, including NASCAR.

No matter where he is, every weekend of Nascar Season, from February through November, he sits in front of the TV watching "the channel" that is broadcasting the latest race. Luke screams at the TV and tells the announcers to shut up and get on with the race.

Luke is a Forever Junior Nation fan all the way! He can spout off driver statistics, car details and who is leading in whatever car series. This is way over my head, but I have such fun watching Luke doing things that he loves to do. The only thing that comes before Nascar in the summer is the weather outside.

For Christmas last year Pat and Bessie bought Luke tickets to see a live Nascar race in Las Vegas, Nevada! Once again, I just cried at this news. It will definitely be a dream come true for Luke, another thing checked off his "bucket list."

Luke's Bump

When you live all your life in a small town, you get to know the area. You know where things are without even knowing the names of the roads. Every winter heading down the off ramp to Palmer, there is a gigantic frost heave that gets bigger and bigger over time. Luke dreads this ginormous bump, which has become enemy number one since his back surgery. He has injured his back several times and worries about it daily. He will remind you EVERY time about the bump. Riding the school bus is even worse. Luke is also very intuitive about people and he can tell if someone is sincere or mean hearted or not understanding. I have gotten in the habit of asking Luke what he thinks about certain people because he is always right.

When he started his junior year, he had a new bus driver who he did not care for from the beginning. He said he was grumpy and drove too fast. Strike one! Heading down the off ramp home after school one afternoon, Luke's bump loomed up ahead and Luke told the bus driver to slow down. Luke said the guy looked right at him and didn't slow down at all. They hit the bump so hard that Luke's wheelchair, all 500+ pounds of it, came up off the floor. Luke came smashing down into his seat and jarred his back. It took several weeks to heal. Strike 2!

The mother bear in me reared her head again and I came unglued. I reported the incident immediately and the bus driver had to attend safety classes all during Christmas break. They even made him sit in a wheelchair blindfolded and drove him around. Ahhh, sweet justice!.

Jello Shooters

Social isolation is one of the challenges Luke has had to face and as a parent, I try to figure out ways for Luke to be included with his peers. Sports, driving and high school parties don't happen for Luke. He is the only student in his entire school who has just a physical disability without other mental or cognitive issues. He is mainstreamed with regular education classes and he has friends, but Luke is never included or invited over to anyone's home and he's left out of trips to the movies or the mall. Most high school students don't have the forethought or resources to include Luke.

Our friends, the Cottinis, completely understand the social isolation issue. Last year on our annual trip to their cabin, someone had the bright idea to make Jello Shooters with peach jello and a little peach schnapps. Luke had one but Glen and his friend Pio did this hilarious act that had Luke believing that they were really drunk. Luke is no dummy, and he immediately realized that he depended on these two men to get him around at the cabin. The two of them actually attach Luke's sling to a metal pole and carry him back and forth between the main house and the guest cabin, where we stay. Pio especially was stumbling around, laughing and joking with everyone. They teased Luke right up until bedtime. Luke was too nice to say anything but his face said it all.

Even after Pio told Luke he was just joking around Luke was still very skeptical. We all tried to help Luke feel more comfortable, but the more we did the more Luke didn't believe us. We were all laughing. Luke laughs about it now and feels incredible that he has friends who try so hard to give him fun experiences.

It wasn't long enough

Luke's first prom was symbolic in that I didn't think I would get to experience seeing him attend. Not only was he attending prom, his date was drop dead gorgeous. I was helping him dress, which was no easy feat with Luke's contractions in his elbows. I could hardly get his arm through the tux jacket sleeve. I helped him with his hair with tears in my eyes, while his dad washed up the van. Luke looked so handsome in his tux.

Before prom, we had decided to take everyone out for dinner at Luke's favorite restaurant, so Bessie, Luke, his date, my daughter and I all piled into the van and headed out. In keeping with the high spirit of the evening, some of us adults ordered drinks while we looked at the menu. The waitress, who seemed very nervous about Luke's wheelchair, came with the drinks and then the unthinkable happened.

She dropped my entire drink all over Luke and his wheelchair. I jumped to action and threw open his tux jacket to hopefully flip off the drink, but his right arm (his driving arm) and joy stick were soaked! I closed my eyes and took a breath so I could get control of my emotions.

I had to take off his jacket, which I barely had gotten on him in the first place, and I wasn't sure if I could get it off with it being wet. I washed his shirt sleeve while it was still on his body but then his arm started getting a rash from the drink and the wheelchair wouldn't turn on. prom was totally not going to happen without his wheelchair. The waitress kept apologizing, saying she would go get the manager. Not only was dinner on the house but they also offered to pay the cleaning bill for the tux. Luke's date was so mad that she ordered the most expensive thing on the menu and shared it with my daughter.

Dinner didn't taste as good as it normally did and frankly, we all thought the night was a bust. I said, "Let's eat and let the joystick dry," while Luke kept telling us that his chair had better turn on. I kept thinking, "Oh please start," but I had no idea what to do if it didn't. I knew we would get home but I wasn't sure if I could help Luke through this disappointment. I joked, saying they wouldn't let

Luke into prom smelling like alcohol. I got a smile out of him but that was it.

To all of our surprise, Luke's chair started! It acted a little strange and Luke said, "I think my wheelchair is a little drunk!" At least his sense of humor and optimism were back! The wheelchair wasn't working perfectly but it seemed good enough to go and his shirt sleeve was almost dry.

I am sure my eyes glistened with moisture as we dropped Luke and his date off at prom. Jenna loved watching the rainbow of pretty dresses. Luke wheeled himself down the corridor and I just smiled, feeling incredible for him. He is the one who wanted to go to prom with or without a date and here he was doing a "normal" teenage thing! I couldn't have been more proud.

When driving home, I could hear the marvel in Luke's voice talking about prom. He said it went by too quickly, even though it was two am by the time we arrived at home. I took his jacket off one more time and I asked him if he had been drinking. He laughed and said "I don't drink and drive."

Chapter Seven

Luke and Ken Summer, 2009

How wonderful to see, other than the wheelchair Luke looks so healthy. Picture taken after Ken the cat decides he would jump up on Luke's lap. It happen so fast Luke was laughing from being startled.

Life Goes On

Luke is a bight individual who is almost always focused on the positive, except when he thinks he has been wronged. He is stubborn when it comes to his care, especially his medical care. He has to be pushed into a corner before he decides anything. Truth be known, I would be the same way. Now that he is older, he thinks things through and is ready to give his opinion when asked. When he gets bored, frustrated or is on a mission, he gets lippy and pushes his limits like any normal teenager. Then the next moment he is completely sharing his love. Every day he tells me he loves me. He can be annoying, argumentative and has a way to drive me straight up the wall! He is insightful and sees beauty all around him and is ready to share it, like the shape of a leaf or the pattern on a waiting room chair that reminds him of a crowd of people.

Sometimes when I am dressing him, the impact of Duchenne on his body sickens me, saddens me, frustrates me and ultimately makes me angry. The feeling is so powerful that I catch myself being rough, impatient and angry. It's like this invisible force takes over and I react and immediately feel guilt and remorse wash through me. I want to be Luke's "rock." During his early teen years, this was almost a daily experience. Now I often go months without an outburst and then his leg will flop a certain way, or his fingers will get stuck, or his sling is difficult to put on, or I spill the pee and snap! I realize now what I feel is normal and when I feel overwhelmed there is usually a very valid reason. I talk with Luke and we figure out the solution together. More times than not it is because I am tired. Initially, it was because I needed more help with Luke's care. I am getting better in how I handle myself and I am able to tell Luke how I am feeling, not to make him feel bad but for him to understand. Luke has a saying, "Communication is Rocket Science." We try very hard to keep the communication open. Sometimes we fail; sometimes we get it right. Isn't that what families do?

As Luke's "care manager," I know Luke's needs, wants and desires. I know his rights and, more importantly, I am his mom and I have every right to make sure that he is taken care of. On the flip side however, I have also made sure that Luke knows how to take care of himself. I have prepared him to think about himself and not expect other people to do things for him. He needs others to take care of his physical needs, but that does not mean that they have a say so over him.

Duchenne sucks but life still goes on, love needs to be shared, bills need to be paid and 365 dinners need to be made a year.

Yard Work

Our summer season in Alaska is only about 12 weeks long. Even into April we still have snow. The minute grass starts poking through here and there Alaskans start spring yard work and the outdoor get-togethers begin. By June and July summer is in full swing and we all pray for the snow to melt off the mountains before the end of August. Sometimes it happens; sometimes we get lucky. One year, my husband cut down some small trees and underbrush in the front of our house to open up the view of Pioneer Peak. Luke and Jenna had this idea that they could use a rope tied to the brush and trees and Luke could pull them over to the burn pile using his wheelchair. I did some but Luke, his aide and Jenna worked on the pile for three or four days. Luke was so proud to be able to do something to help out around the house.

Hell And Back

It was the last week of August 2009 and the sun was shining, no wind whipped the tips of the leaves that were just starting to turn yellow and that meant a perfect day for a buggy trip. We headed up to the Jonesville Coal Mine Road to check out part of the trail we hadn't seen in some time. It was a glorious day and we stopped and ate lunch, viewed wild mountain goats through the scope, and explored old drill holes made by the coal miners back in the day when they used to dynamite the mountain.

As usual, we waved at all the other locals enjoying what would most likely be the last summer day we would have for seven long months. As we were leaving, Glen noticed a trail leading off through a man-made canyon wall and decided we should go check it out. On the side of one wall someone had sprayed painted the words "Welcome to Hell," in graffiti-like letters. We just laughed and thought, yeah right, scary!

Once in the canyon, we saw these two guys, one driving through this large mud hole on a four wheeler covered from head to toe in mud and the other filming his buddy tearing up the mud hole, sending clumps of mud and water flying. We watched them and thought we would have no problem having some fun in that mud ourselves.

Glen drove into the mud hole slowly and everything seemed fine. Wrong! Suddenly we felt the buggy sink right up to the frame, tires turning like large, useless chocolate donuts. Normally I would be doing the freaked out mom thing but all I could do was laugh and grab my mud boots. We had to figure out how in the heck we were going to get out of this mess!

We always take a winch with us but as we looked around, we noticed that there were absolutely no trees anywhere close enough for us to use. Thankfully about 100 yards away there were some large boulders. We slowly winched the buggy out with big, slurpy mud sounds the entire way. Luke is a chip off the old block and was so calm in his faith that Glen would get us out of there. We took a picture of the graffiti on our way out. Whoever wrote those words weren't kidding! Welcome to hell alright!

Don't Die Without Me

Two weeks after the homecoming dance, Luke and 400 other students ended up with the flu. Young men with DMD are respiratory impaired, so this illness landed Luke in the hospital for nine days.

Prior to what we fondly refer to as "Luke's vacation" was a week of three emergency room visits, major sleep deprivation, high stress and me being scared out of my mind. Luke had a fever, he wouldn't eat, his heart rate was through the roof and he was more stubborn about going to the doctor than I had ever seen him before.

Outwardly, Jenna seemed to be doing fine. She prayed for Luke every night but she seemed well otherwise. I finally put my foot down after several days of this and told Luke that he had no choice: We were heading into Anchorage to the Providence Hospital. His in-home care support person loaded the van and I went to the bathroom when the phone rang. Luke can't pick up the phone on his own, so the recorder came on. It was Jenna, crying, and saying "Mom, I really need to talk to you, pick up the phone, I am scared, I don't want Luke to die without me." With my heart crumbling into a million pieces yet again, I came out of the bathroom to find Luke moved emotionally. He had tears in his eyes when he said, "I didn't realize how worried she was."

Hospital Blessing

Luke was admitted to the hospital immediately. He was dehydrated and his potassium level was dangerously low. Low potassium causes lack of appetite and lactic acid build up in the muscles, causing the body to hurt all over. He also had the flu and pneumonia. They told us that he would most likely have long term respiratory damage, which meant we should be thinking about a tracheotomy. This was never an option that we even wanted to consider. I so wanted Luke to finish high school without any major medical issues. I was super emotional and in mother bear mode. I held it together for Luke, but once I left the room to talk on the phone or take a walk, I would break-down. I was scared for Luke, for Jenna and the rest of the family.

After three days spent at the hospital, I was exhausted and just wanted to sleep on the makeshift pull- out bed that I had made beside Luke's bed. The doctor had told him that if he used his cough assist machine with the respiratory team every hour on the hour to cough out the fluid in his lungs, he could go home. This was all Luke needed to hear. He put his entire being into following the doctor's orders. He coughed every hour on the hour for a day and a half until he couldn't cough anymore. Watching him put his mind to something and fight is a memory imprinted in my mind for life. I swell with pride thinking about how hard he worked and, at the same time, it made me indescribably sad. I could not do this for him. I could not take his pain away this time. I had to force myself to remember that if you help a butterfly out of its cocoon, it will die.

As I lay there praying for sleep to take me for a few hours, Luke just would not stop talking. Looking back on it, I am pretty sure he thought that if he kept talking, nothing bad was going to happen to him. I kept thinking, "Please Luke, shut up! I need some rest." After a few minutes of silence, he said "Mom are you asleep yet?" I said, "No," and what he said next melted my heart. He said, "I love you Mom, I don't know what I would do without you." I am so glad that I stayed awake long enough to hear such heavenly words. I cried and said, "I know".

My sister had been driving an hour almost every day to visit either before work or after. One day before she left she asked if we could all pray together. The blessing she gave was from the heart and touched both Luke and me deeply. Luke said he felt very much loved and that everything was going to be okay. He also said that, in a way, our hospital vacation had been kind of fun. I said, minus the stress it was fun, just he and I hanging out, watching movies but more importantly having time with just the two of us. Our human-to-human, friend to friend, mother to child bond became stronger than ever. I wouldn't call myself a religious person but I am deeply spiritual. I believe we are all connected. Everything happens for a reason, even though events don't always make sense at the moment they occur. Life is an amazing journey full of transformation and awakening. But the religious blessing from my sister that day brought me such comfort and peace that I want to share it. I am truly grateful for it.

> Father God, I first want to start off by thanking
> You for blessing us with Luke. Lord,
> You knew what You were doing when You sent
> him into our lives! I have learned
> From Luke to treat each day as it's your last and
> to live it up! He is SO strong and I know
> that only comes from You. Father as Luke and Misty
> face this next step in life,
> Lord I ask for Your direction. I ask that
> You would be with the doctors, give them
> the knowledge and wisdom to know what to do next.
> Lord bless them for all that they do. Father I ask that
> You would direct both Luke and
> Misty and help them make the right medical choice for Luke.
> Father you are an amazing
> God and the great physician. I ask that Your will,
> will be done in this situation and rest to come when it
> comes to Luke's life.
> Father give Luke the rest he needs to heal and
> help him to stay strong. Lord I again praise
> Your name for Luke and the blessing I have to be his aunt.
> Lord. You are in control and I ask that You would give
> Misty and Luke the peace of knowing that.
> I say these things in Your glorious and
> precious name. Amen

My Doggie

We'd barely been home a week from "Luke's Vacation" when Glen came in from feeding our dog, Max, and said that he wasn't eating. I called our vet, who is a family friend, and she came over for a home visit the next day. We ended up taking him to her clinic for x-rays and we discovered that his bladder was as big as a watermelon, pushing his intestines up toward his heart. The outlook was not good for our beloved pet of 13 years and we decided to put him down. I took him home to spend some time with Luke and Jenna before the vet come to euthanize him.

The yellow and orange leaves of fall were all over the ground next to his dog house where he spent his final minutes in my arms. Jenna sat on top of the dog house and Luke sat nearby as Max took his last breaths. I was crying, Jenna was crying, then Luke started crying. This was all it took for the vet to start crying. We were all blubbering like big babies. Max was part of the family. Luke, trying to be the tough man, finally broke down and sobbed, "My doggie!"

Class Ring

"Can you believe your boy is a Senior, Mom?" Luke asked me coming into the house after school recently. I simply answered "No," but in my mind I wondered if he knew the significance of his words. He then said, "Guess what? I brought home all of the order forms for my cap and gown, but you can order the ring online. It's so cool! You can even design it on a website!" Luke bugged me all night, so finally I caved in. He was right, it was very cool and it only took about 30 minutes for us to design the ring he wanted.

I told Luke I wasn't going to wear any makeup for graduation because all was going to do was cry the entire time. I never thought I would be see him graduate. I had prepared myself during all of these years that he might be gone by the time most kids graduate and here we were, just four months away from the big day. Luke says he is sad to leave behind his teachers, aides and therapists. He also says he feels like he just started high school because it's only been two years since he was mainstreamed.

Advocating

Since recently taking charge of his life, Luke says he has woken up to the real world. I couldn't be more proud of him. I consider Luke living to 18 and, experiencing graduation with him to be one of the life's highest honors. What a wonderful sight to witness Luke training his own aides and support people, taking care of his own scheduling and remembering everything he needs to transport himself from one household to the other. He keeps us all on our toes and is always thinking ahead and looking on the bright side. Luke is Mr. Positive ninety percent of the time and he has a great outlook on life. He loves his life, his family and has dreams for the future. He plans to take AutoCAD since he loves to design and create things. Alaska is a young state and it is one of the few that is growing, so AutoCAD will come in handy when he starts looking for a job. He actually already has a job with an engineering firm and he hasn't even taken a lick of college. And oh, did I mention, Luke is a poet.

This Place

When Luke was first diagnosed I used to go to a place where I'd walk through fields of vegetables and nap in grassy meadows with the power and energy of majestic mountains standing like protective giants of my mind, body and spirit. A place where I could rejuvenate my heart and soul. I needed to be with what I knew was real, what I could see, what I could touch and smell. The earth, the sunshine, the gentle breeze on my face. It is the place I was born and now the place where I live, laugh and love. The place where Glen grew up and then to which he introduced me and offered to share. A place Luke instantly fell in love with as a little boy. VanderWeele Farms spoke to my heart the very first time I set foot on her fields, took in the beauty of her scenery and the glory of Pioneer Peak.

Luke wrote this poem for his poetry class which showcases perfectly what the farm means to him.

"This Place"

There is a place on the farm
To get away from it all
This place has a certain charm
Open and free with no walls
Green rows that go on for miles
Topped with white flowers so high
A landscape so beautiful and wild
Yet not like the days gone by
Surrounding the field of green and white
A dirt road weaves and whines
Standing tall the fireweed is such a sight
A more perfect place is hard to find
The irrigation sprinklers spray the mist
The heat of the day shines down from above
The water beads on leaves it's kissed
And moistens the ground that was tilled with love
Such a sunny day with puffy white clouds
A slight breeze sings through the leaves
Of trees that stand so tall and proud
And still so much more to see
With Pioneer Peak rising to the sky
What an incredible and glorious day

An eagle soars on wings so high
This place just takes your breath away!

Let There Be Light

January brings bitter cold, clear blue nights. Often the fog will settle over the land as it did just a few short months ago, frosting the trees and anything else in its path. On one such night recently, I was sitting by the Christmas tree looking out at it all. The moon was out, sending its glow over the ice crystals that had gathered on the deck. They sparkled like a field of diamonds. As if reading my mind, Luke said from behind me, "Aren't they beautiful, Mom?" I, of course, replied "yes they are, son." The meaning of Luke is: He who brings light. What a fitting name for my son, for it is absolutely true.

Chapter Eight

VanderWeele Farms, aka: This Place
Every time I see this picture I want to take a walk. This is the view I see every day.

I am completely blessed to not only be Luke's mom but to be his friend. Over the years we have been put in circumstances where I had to be so much more than a "normal mom." I am his confidant, a person he can be who he is with, a person he has gone the distance with, and a person who has stood by his side during the horrors of Duchenne.

With each stage of this disease, there are lots of little deaths, each bringing new grief, new fears, new challenges and having to let go of "once was." From walking to using a wheelchair, from being able to dress yourself to someone else having to do it for you, from being able to bring the fork to your mouth to having to be fed. The simple things we take for granted disappear. It's often like taking one step forward and three steps back. The three steps back always taking you to the very same place. Duchenne Muscular Dystrophy is stealing your son's life. Somehow you have to go on with each downward progression to find the life balance that each of us desires without being swallowed whole from the sheer and ever present, agonizing grief. I have often wondered when is it ever going to end just to realize if it did Luke wouldn't be here. Yes, Duchenne sucks! So now what?

"Here I am Living For Today...But I'm Gonna Hope for Tomorrow" Excerpt from the song "The Innocence" by: Duchenne Music Project.

Hope is what you have before dreams and miracles become reality. Now is the time to do, to take action, to push and live ONWARD!

At this very moment there are boys and young men dying of Duchenne. There are also boys and young men living. Some even improving their symptoms of Duchenne. With treatments that for some reason are being hush hushed. I do understand we must make sure that treatments are safe and viable. It's hard to make rash decisions when our sons' lives are at stake, but isn't it high time to put the cure for Duchenne on the map?

With hesitant excitement Luke will be receiving his first STS treatment by Dr. Rhodes in June. It's a relatively new, innovative treatment that works at the cellular level, with no harmful side effects. If I had it my way, I would put Luke on the first plane out of Alaska. But Luke has decided to finish his senior year and graduate in May. He told me, "I need to put graduation behind me and the treatment will give me something to look forward to."

Does this scare me? Absolutely! But I force myself every day not to dwell on the negative. It is uncharted territory. Polio is a thing of the past and the cancer that President Carter declared war on is being cured every day. What can't be done is always being done by someone, so why not a cure for Duchenne?

Below is an email I received from some dear friends of mine. I was expressing to them my fear of getting excited about this new treatment.

This email is their response:

Hi Misty,

Go ahead and get excited. You have committed your heart already

(with some reservation, but you committed it when you decided to try this).

Faith and hope is the other part of the equation that makes any healing work.

If it doesn't work, then that is what you have us for. You can rant and rave

your frustrations and disappointments on us!

We pray that this new strategy will work, but why not expect miracles? I know that you have hoped against hope many times before, and have had some successes and some failures. In this world we do know miracles happen. They are rare, so we tend to think we are not worthy of them. That is correct logic, for none of us are worthy of them - even those who have had the miracles! Miracles have happened to those without hope, without conscious belief, but that is even rarer. Go ahead and hope (with some reservation, but recognize it is hope). Get excited (with some reservation, but get excited). The last verse in 1 Corinthians 13 says that "these three remain, faith, hope, and love, but the greatest of these is love." I know you already "love" so you already have the greatest ingredient for a miracle to happen.

The next is to simply believe the impossible. That is why we are all fools, but it is better to be a fool with hope, than a wise person in despair.

Despair gets little done and is our biggest enemy...

We love you all and share in your hopes and your dreams.

We have some reservations, too, but we are excited!

Tim and Kelly Caraway

Will the treatment work? I must believe and "know" it will. High emotional stakes are at risk. For my husband who wants to fix this for Luke but can't. For Luke's siblings who cherish the ground he wholes his wheelchair on. For the family, for Luke's dad's family, for my daughter, who had this to say about the treatment: "You mean that Luke could one day hug me back?"

And for me, although there is a certain amount of comfort and "normalness" in living this long with Duchenne. I am thrilled to be in this spot, living and watching Luke live. But I have to admit it scares the absolute shit out of me to change the dance steps and head into the uncharted territory of Luke living a very long time. Have I done what is best for Luke? Have I taught him enough about self-advocacy for him to be able to live an independent life?

Unequivocally YES! Why, because that is what moms do.

In Your Face, Duchenne Muscular Dystrophy, All Pain...All GLORY!

I Did It

I made my way through the crowd of happy graduates, balloons, and streamers to find Luke. I knew he'd be having a hard time trying to drive his wheelchair through the mass. I spotted him from a distance and just watched the look on his face. It was one of bewilderment and astonishment that he had actually graduated high school with a diploma. He looked so proud. I ran over to him with proud mama tears and he kept saying to me, "Mom, I DID IT! MOM I DID IT!"

Eyes Like Saucers

After the arduous 16 hour trip from Alaska to Texas with a 350 pound power wheelchair, which included two airport connections, a constipation turned diarrhea issue, and a hotel reservation mess-up, we finally arrived at the clinic to learn all about the STS treatment. Duchenne had taken so much of Luke's body by this point. He couldn't move his legs and had very little control over his feet. The only real movement besides his head came from his fingers and hands. He had to spider crawl his fingers to his wheelchair joystick or ask someone to place his hand so he could drive. We were looking at the treatment as any healing would be good healing.

About 20 minutes into his very first treatment, all of sudden Luke's eyes grew big as saucers. I jumped up asking, "What's wrong?" After a few moments of shock, he said, "I CAN BREATHE!" I said, "Well, that is a good thing." He laughed and said, "I can breathe with *all* my lungs." Then he sneezed a few times., which he hadn't done in a very long time. This was huge, as breathing issues are often a problem for Duchenne patients. We were excited. We had hope. We had each other. Later Luke cried and said, "You guys don't understand. I never thought I could feel this way again."

On days 2 and 3 things got even more impressive. Luke had finished his night time treatment and his sister leaned over. She put his arm around her neck and he gave her a squeeze. The squeezing wasn't something Luke could do prior to treatment. They both were practically in tears; we all were. This was the first hug she had ever received from her big brother. It was one incredible moment of many on that trip.

Superman Syndrome

Once back home, Luke's dedication to doing two 80 minute treatments a day was impressive. I don't think I had ever seen him this happy before. Also his energy level and increased mobility were a sight for sore eyes. I remember asking him one time, "What if the treatment stopped working?" He replied, "At least I got to try it. It made me feel good while it lasted." His positivity was inspiring.

The only negative, if I can call it that, was that Luke felt so good he was pushing himself. He had his aide drive him all over to his favorite spots across the valley we live in. He kept up with all his physical and occupational therapies. He was always going, going, going. It was incredible and scary to watch at the same time. I called it Superman Syndrome. It was the first time he actually felt like he had a chance at a future and he wasn't going to miss any of it.

At one point he decided to move in to his Dad's place, as his dad had newly refurbished and made accessible Luke's very own room and mini apartment. The idea that it would give more privacy and a better sense of independence he craved. I didn't want him to leave full time but understood this was something he really wanted to do. The downside was that Luke replaced all of the caregivers and agencies I had set up for him. He started over from square one. Hindsight revealed that he put himself directly into a lot of stress because he wanted to prove that he could do it on his very own. It broke my heart to see him go, but I let him. Not that I could or would have stopped him anyway. I didn't know what the future would bring. And a part of me was relieved as well. I was tired and stressed from taking care of him, and I'd just written and published two books in two years and was working on number three. I thought I'd use this time to take care of myself. Luke promised he'd check in and that we'd still have family time. And we did.

I Need Your Help

Seven months later, the stress of doing it all and trying to treat his constipation by taking laxatives every day (which I had no knowledge of) took its toll. He came to me asking for help and to see if he could move back in, as he ended up having major weight loss that broke my heart.

Just like breathing issues often cause Duchenne patients to receive tracheotomies, eating and weight issues often cause them to need feeding tubes. I knew Luke wouldn't go for the tube. After talking to the doctor, we put Luke on a 2000 calorie a day diet, including a food journal which Luke was diligent about. I never had to remind him. He cracked the whip and had us all in line.

When he moved back in, it was super stressful as I was in the middle of another book launch and I had commandeered his room as my office.

Again, hindsight is 20/20. I now believe his body was too fragile for such a heavy food load and that it really put extra strain on his colon. But he did gain a bit of weight back and was doing much better for a while. It looked like things were on the up and up.

Let's Do it Right Here

A construction company was building these fun little cottage homes right up the road from our house. I knew one of Luke's dreams was to have his own home. One day I saw one of their trucks parked out in front of one of the houses. I stopped in to ask some questions about what it would take to get Luke one of his own. The owner said,

"Let's do it right here. I'll come over soon and get together with Luke to go over the floor plan that would best suit his needs."

Luke's move-in date was set for October. Luke was ecstatic; he drove over there every day to check on the progress. They called him Boss. And they had a surprise for Luke. They were all working a little extra on the unit that was to be Luke's place. Luke wound up being able to make the move in August, a full two months before he thought! We worked like crazy to get him interviewed and approved care staff and somehow made it work.

One Stressed Out Mama

20 years of worry, stress, hospital stays, surgeries, and too many sleepless nights to count were finally catching up to me. I was so exhausted but kept pushing, not that I could have stopped taking care of Luke if I had wanted to.

My first round of shingles was miserable, my second round had me on the couch for three days in extreme pain, and the fourth time had me running the doctor to get my own STS, now called the Vector machine. Which, thank goodness, heals them faster.

However, having shingles wipes me out. I feel incredibly ill, nerves shot, not to mention so emotional and sensitive that crying can start over seemingly nothing. I'm also one of the lucky ones who gets shingles on my face. Very painful!

This was also the time when life seemed to bring on crisis after crisis that needed my attention. I remember the look of worry on Luke's face. I could tell he felt bad that I had to take care of him, especially with me being so sick.

Three Books In One

As I said in the introduction this book is actually three books in one. The third book is **Heart Shaped Rocks**, which shares how my son's life impacted my daughter Jenna's. Although *Heart Shaped Rocks* overlaps the timeline of *In Your Face* a little it will give you a deeper understanding into the story as a whole. You could skip it, but you'd be missing out on a lotta love.

Introduction

Heart Shaped Rocks is a story in progress. It is my daughter Jenna's story, a living story which unfolds little by little every day. You see, Jenna, like tens of thousands of other siblings, has spent her first 14 years on this planet knowing that her brother could die at any moment from complications of Duchenne Muscular Dystrophy.

Duchenne Muscular Dystrophy, or simply Duchenne or DMD as it is commonly referred to, is the most common form of muscular dystrophy. It is a muscle wasting disease which mainly affects boys, although girls can be diagnosed with it too. Its victims, like my son Luke, are born seemingly healthy, but as time goes on and the disease progresses, the body's muscles get thinner and weaker, eventually rendering the child unable to walk. By the age of 10 or 12 a Duchenne child must use an electric wheelchair for mobility. A manual wheelchair isn't practical since he is usually too weak to propel himself. At the same time Duchenne takes away lower body strength, it starts affecting upper body strength, eventually destroying the heart and lungs which results in premature death in young adulthood, usually by the late teens or mid-twenties.

When Jenna was born, her brother, Luke, was able to hold and feed her. In her toddler years she rode on the back of his electric wheelchair. By the time she was in elementary school, Luke was not able to lift his arms to hug her or even give her a brotherly slug in the arm. Although Jenna's story of life as a Duchenne sibling is heartbreaking, I want you to know that like my first book, In Your Face Duchenne Muscular Dystrophy, All Pain...All GLORY!, this book is about making the very most out of what life throws at you while looking for those synchronistic signs and Aha moments that teach you that life is meant to be lived on purpose. This time, instead of telling the story of my son's battle with DMD, my intention is to honor my daughter's life as she watches how much Duchenne takes from her brother, while at the same time benefiting from all that it gives in terms of passion, maturity, and strength of character.

As her mother, it's an honor to witness the transformation of a young girl into the young woman Jenna is becoming. She has so much to offer this world. Just wait until you read how on purpose and full of love for life Jenna is and how Duchenne has molded her. Living in the face of uncertainty has helped her develop into a young lady submerged in love for life, compassion, and the example of living grace. She gives her heart gently, but full on. I am sure you'll fall in love with her one heart shaped rock at a time.

Heart Shaped Rocks follows my son, Luke's, progression with Duchenne starting with my pregnancy with Jenna, all the way to the present day with Jenna now being 14 years old. It details her journey as Duchenne ravages her brother's body and then takes his life. You will be moved by Jenna over and over as you read about the love they shared. But first let me give you some background with which to lay out her story.

As a Duchenne carrier, I have a 50% chance of having a child born with Duchenne. And as I mentioned earlier, Duchenne mostly affects boys but girls can have it too (although that's very rare). So when my son was diagnosed back in 1994 I had decided there would be no more children for me. At that time I had just started a relationship with my now husband Glen and we decided that having one child would be enough for both of us. Besides, I knew what was to come in the future and I wasn't too sure I wanted to put this kind of grief into another person's life, let alone another child. However, life had a surprise in store for us.

That surprise was Jenna.

Although having another child wasn't planned and often left me worried about the future, I knew it was supposed to be or it wouldn't be happening in the first place. There are almost 8 years between Luke and Jenna. This means their sibling relationship is unique. Luke was the typical protective big brother, but as time went on and Luke started losing more of his physical ability, Jenna would step in and be his hands, arms, and feet. They would roam the fields of the farm where we live, Jenna his photographer and he the director. She would sit long hours and watch him play video games and fetch his water when he asked. Their mutual admiration was always felt. They would squabble now and again, but what siblings don't? Watching their interaction with each other always brought me such joy, with a little sadness around the edges if I thought about a future without Luke in it and how that would affect Jenna.

During the writing of this book, we laid Jenna's brother, to rest in a beautiful cemetery with the view of what Luke referred to as his mountains. Currently, I live, work and play with my daughter, Jenna, and my husband, Glen, on his family's vegetable farm here in Alaska. It's an incredible lifestyle to be a part of, with all the fresh air, vegetables and scenery. Most people don't know but Alaska got started with agriculture back in 1935 through President Roosevelt's resettlement program. Although many farms are not in operation anymore, there are a handful of farmers left. Some of us are lobbying for Alaska to be a self-sustainable state. We live in a vast valley surrounded by mountains and glaciers. Our home in particular has an incredible view and numerous fields to roam, which we enjoy frequently. It's an incredible place to raise a family and grow a happy life. It's one of many things I am in awe of; I feel deeply grateful to get to live here and I embrace all that this home-spun family-farm lifestyle has to offer.

So what does Heart Shaped Rocks have to do with living in the face of Duchenne? Well, you will learn just that as you continue to turn the pages of this book.

Preface

What a fortunate teacher I am that Jenna VanderWeele and her family came into my life. I feel incredibly honored to be a contributing member of this book about such a wonderful kid.

Jenna and I first met in the spring quarter of her 3rd grade year when I occasionally helped out in her reading class. She was quick, funny and very direct! I learned soon after that Jenna was often worried about her older brother Luke's health. She carried this around in the most heartfelt way, was leery about sharing this news with just anyone and would sometimes break down into tears if pushed too far. She was still working through so much of the world happening around her. When the school year ended I hoped that our paths would cross again. And, to my good fortune, they did!

The following fall, Jenna was placed in my 4th grade classroom! I've always enjoyed Jenna and was so pleased we would be continuing our learning together. We had a great time that year, teaching one another about love, light, PEACE and laughter! When I moved up to teach 5th grade the following year I was allowed to take a few kids with me. Jenna was on the list! This was wonderful for us both as I grew closer to her mom, met her Dad and of course, her brother, Luke.

Luke's health was a main priority with Jenna and her family, which was all encompassing for them. When Luke was doing well, they all were. If he had moments of caution, the family all worked together, pulled up their bootstraps and met the challenge head on. At school, Jenna might've been having the best of days, until she wasn't....those moments were especially tough on Jenna. So I would ask her out into the hall so that she could take some gentle time to breathe, and calm herself down with plenty of hugs before she could get on with her day.

Jenna's compassion, grit and humor are such worthy qualities for someone so young. She and Luke shared so much of their humor together. Her compassion comes from the heart and has been within her the whole time. Her grit comes from her parents' ability to put one foot in front of the other to keep going through the trials and tribulations that families face with Duchenne Muscular Dystrophy.

When Luke passed away, it was a very difficult time but the family's strength comes from an undying support of one another. The memorial was well attended by family and friends and the reception was an amazing, true testament of Luke's life. Jenna thoroughly enjoyed the moment with reminders of Luke's amazing life all around her. The family celebrates him daily knowing that while Luke is enjoying absolutely no boundaries; his gift to them includes the freedom for them to wander to many new horizons.

Misty has done an excellent job of writing how the moments in Luke's life affected Jenna and those around her. Jenna misses Luke terribly, but keeps her head high and delves into life looking for kindness and beauty everywhere she can. I smiled a lot when I read Misty's words. Jenna still gives 'everything' a name, takes in life at school, her home, loves her animals and often surprises us with her own simplistic ideas to solve the discussion at hand. Yes, and heart shaped rocks never go unnoticed!

Enjoy this read. It comes from the loving heart of a mom and a great family I am proud to know.

I anxiously look forward to watching Jenna grow into the amazing young woman I know she will be.

-Kathleen R. Jones
a.k.a. "The Peace Teacher"

Chapter One: The Heart of the Matter

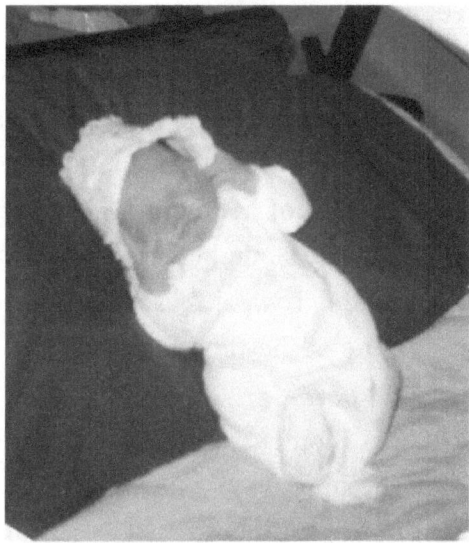

"The most beautiful things in the world cannot be seen or even touched, they must be felt with the heart." ~ Helen Keller

God wouldn't give me more than I could handle, right?

I used to have this idea that my son being dealt the hand of Duchenne was the end of all my troubles, or at least that no new ones would appear. I believed that somehow I would get through this tragedy, help a bunch of other people in the process, and then get on with life. Yes, it would hurt like hell, but other parents had learned to go on after the death of a child. I figured I'd find a way to survive one way or another. For a while I also bought into the "there's nothing we can do so go home and enjoy your son while you still have him" mentality hook, line and sinker.

The God wouldn't give me more than I could handle saying was almost my mantra. I had absolutely no idea that once you start on the

Duchenne journey, you are on the journey for life. Let's just say I didn't get the memo.

"You're pregnant."

WHAT? This question screamed in my mind. I knew I hadn't been feeling well, but pregnant? No way was this happening. What was I going to tell Glen? We weren't even married yet. I knew that he hadn't wanted any children of his own; he had told me so. Luke was newly diagnosed with an incurable disease, and worse, this baby could have Duchenne too! I was just sick inside from this news. My friend who was with me at the time later told me I looked like I had just seen a ghost.

All I knew at that moment was that I would keep this baby no matter what. I took the long way home to absorb this new change in my life before springing the news on Glen. I was pretty sure that Luke, who was 7 at the time, would be okay with the news, probably even excited. I also knew I had to be certain in my heart about what I was going to do, no matter what Glen decided.

If you read my first book, In Your Face, you know that Glen chose us, knowing that Luke had Duchenne, knowing there was a possibility the new baby could have Duchenne and all. We got married and committed to create the best life possible for our family. Luke was the ring bearer and both my boys wore mud flaps (what Glen told Luke the tails of their tuxedoes were).

Little Bird

After the initial shock of actually being pregnant wore off, I had this internal "knowing" the baby I was carrying was a girl. For obvious reasons besides already having a boy, I knew I needed this baby to be a girl. I wasn't so sure I could handle another blow. Her name was already Jenna, which means little bird. I was about 7 months along and even with all the previous ultrasounds, we couldn't tell the sex of the baby. My anxiety was high as I worried that my gut feelings might be wrong. I kept second guessing myself until one spring morning. I had been up all night with worry the night before. I had asked God to give me a sign if I was right about this baby being a girl. I got my answer.

I was getting ready to leave for my last ultrasound after working in our greenhouse that day. And up in the tree was this lone "little bird" singing its heart out. I cried all the way to the ultrasound appointment and when the doctor asked me if I knew the sex of the baby, I said, "She's a girl."

"Are you okay?"

Jenna was born on a sunny July morning. I immediately fell in love with her as she nursed and gazed into my eyes for the very first time. She was the most beautiful baby I'd ever seen. She was an angel. All of a sudden up high on the left side of my body, in the high lung upper throat area, was this intense pain that made me very uncomfortable. I felt like I had swallowed something entirely too big. One nurse asked me if I was okay. I said "Yes, but I have this horrible pain," and I grabbed where the pain was coming from. They whisked Jenna away from me. They gave me a shot of blood thinners and had me hooked up to almost every machine they had. I came to find out I had a pulmonary embolism, which means I had a blood clot in my lungs. They were very worried the clot would travel either to my brain or my heart. Although I was scared, I had my baby girl, my wonderful husband, and an incredible son with an uncertain future who needed me.

I had found a life I had never dreamed of and I wasn't going anywhere!

Cheerio O's

We brought her home in a white eyelet lace baby bonnet. Over the next month of newborn-ness Jenna would make these O's with her mouth as she looked around. She was often referred to as pumpkin, turnip, and pickle as each of us had our own vegetable names for her. She was the highlight of our lives, our "little sprout". For her first Halloween we dressed her up as a baby leopard, black nose and all. Then the first Christmas came. We were totally enamored with her.

Whirlwind

Great Grandma Mary from Texas called Jenna "a little whirlwind" as Jenna ran through the house never missing a beat. And her Great Oma on Glen's side would marvel over how determined she was to learn new things. However, I was starting to notice her not so fun trait of being overly sensitive and whiny over small things. This forced me to change my parenting style since she'd throw a fit from the pressure of not only wanting to do good, but not wanting to do what was expected or being asked. On one hand I knew that being a sensitive person is a gift, but on the other I worried how we were going to handle it as she got older.

Furniture to Furniture

As most babies do before they start to walk, Jenna found comfort and more freedom going from furniture to furniture. She was thrilled to be standing on her own and taking her first steps. This is also when the progression of her brother's disease started to become more apparent. At 8 years old he reverted to the comfort and safety of going from one piece of furniture to the next. As Jenna started walking, her brother was taking his last steps. We knew the electric wheelchair wasn't too far ahead.

Brotherly Love

Luke was proud of Jenna; he loved her and continually showed his affection. There wasn't too much jealousy on his part. Maybe it was the years between them. Whatever it was, he felt very protective of her. I'd take him to her doctor's appointments with me. He would watch them like a hawk just waiting for them to mess up. Nobody was going to hurt his baby sister!

Road Kill

The toddler years – and yes, Luke's first wheelchair – found Jenna wanting to be a part of Luke's every waking moment. She loved riding on the back of his wheelchair and taking whatever Luke was using or playing with and running away. She knew Luke couldn't catch her. She would squeal and run. Luke would get fed up and tell her she was going to be "road kill." There was no way Luke was ever going to hurt her. He was always fearful of running over her anyway. But kids will be kids, and the empty threat was what he had to work with.

Shared Custody

Luke's dad would come and pick him up for his two weeks. When Jenna was a baby she would cry and cry seeing her brother leave. As his disease progressed, the two weeks turned into a time for doing things her brother physically couldn't, and a time for resting up until he came home again. It was a time for her to be just Jenna.

Chapter Two: Have a Heart

"Where so ever you go, go with all your heart." ~ Unknown

During these years our main focus was giving Luke the best life we could while living, working, and taking care of his physical needs. There was always a lot of love with a big dose of fear. But we did the best we could, and looking back, probably better than a lot of people do without living in the face of Duchenne Muscular Dystrophy. Jenna was just as swept up in it as we were. It's not like she had a choice, but she never complained and simply accepted that this was her life. She gave her love and support easily and would even put herself on the back burner, not wanting to rock the boat. However, being so young and living such an emotional roller coaster 24/7, her feelings had to come out somehow.

As the toddler years ended, through pre-school and on into grade school Jenna's personality started to emerge. My beautiful, determined whirlwind started to become increasingly volatile and extremely emotional over the littlest things. At one point I remember thinking, what happened to my little girl? I was very concerned for her, especially when her classmates started calling her a crybaby. Jenna would still have moments of being her on-purpose self, then with a flip of a switch she became a whiny, crying, hesitant, almost fearful child. In public she'd become a real handful. I could see and feel other mothers pass judgment on her. I was at a loss for how to help my pumpkin pie.

I've heard it said that when there are problems with a child, you should look to the child's home life. The fact was her brother was losing his independence and having to go through surgeries, and would become sick easily. The daily fear of living knowing her brother could die was taking its toll, not just on her but on me. I was torn. I knew we wouldn't have Luke with us forever and I didn't want us as a family to miss one moment. I wanted Jenna to be included all the way. I was plagued with thoughts like Jenna is just as important as Luke. How am I going to live in fear of losing my son and still be the mother my daughter needs me to be? Because obviously what I was doing wasn't working.

I decided to do what I always do when I'm backed into a corner. I start asking for a sign telling me what to do. Believe me when I say, I got many of them!

He Found His Way Back to Her

Jenna loves animals with her whole heart. We already had Max, the family dog, but I felt that Jenna needed a kitty of her very own. So when I heard about free farm kitties up the road it was perfect timing. Having something to love and take care of seemed just the right thing for her. What was even more perfect was that she was able to have the pick of the litter. Jenna's only requirement was that she wanted a girl cat. She picked a cute little friendly fuzzy orange tabby kitty. The owners said it was a girl, but I didn't think orange tabby cats were ever females. I kept quiet until we had to take Kloe to the vet for her first shots. When we came in, the lady at the desk said, "Do you know Kloe is a boy?" I thought, oh no, time for a meltdown. Nope, Jenna didn't miss a beat: "Well then his name has to be Ken." The gal and I looked at each other. Jenna put her hand on her hip and said, "You know, Barbie and KEN?" Whew, what a relief. Well, about a month later Ken got out of our van somehow when we were at Luke's physical therapy appointment, about 3 miles from home. We searched all over for him. I was so afraid to tell Jenna that I had lost her cat. I cried all the way home to tell her. Just like I thought, she cried herself to sleep that night, and the next. I felt horrible. On the third night I heard a squeaking sound on the glass patio doors. It was KEN! I couldn't believe it. I scooped him up and put him in bed with Jenna. She was overjoyed that he had found his way back to her.

Brownies

I was still looking for signs about what I needed to do to help Jenna when she came home wanting to join girl scouts. But there was a catch. There happened to be too many girls and not enough leaders. Here was something Jenna wanted to do and it looked like if I didn't step up and be the leader she wouldn't get to be a part of it. I couldn't let that happen. I remember driving away after signing up to be a girl scout leader thinking, what did I just do? Okay God, I'm listening. You know with Luke's care I hardly have time for much else. I was scared and excited all at the same time but I knew this was the sign I needed. I knew Jenna needed to be a part of something outside the home, something just for her. We were already trying ballet, soccer, basketball... nothing was working. But what was different about girl scouts is that Jenna and I were doing it together. Although I had no idea how to be a girl scout leader I had 7 little girls wanting to become brownies. It was fun doing art projects, going on field trips and jamborees. And let's not forget the girl scout cookies. Jenna was still emotional but we were making progress. I could tell she liked me being her girl scout leader. But something still wasn't right. I just couldn't put my finger on it.

Caregiver Nightmare

Something had happened to my Jenna and her brother that I was unaware of. It didn't come out until the year she joined girl scouts but it reveals more about why my sweet girl was often times an emotional wreck. A care provider of Luke's was terrorizing my children by making them watch bloody scary movies and then she'd lock Jenna in her room. It was horrifying! We were unable to bring charges against the care provider. Jenna went from being able to sleep in the dark to needing a night light and not sleeping well. Luckily this care provider was only in our house a couple of months. However, the damage had been done.

Her Gift

Starting in preschool and continuing through grade school teachers would tell me how compassionate and helpful Jenna was toward others, and then almost in the same breath they would say – "But we have been dealing with her tears and crying in the class room." After one such meeting when Jenna got into the van, she seemed quiet so I asked her if anything was wrong. Tears instantly sprang to her eyes as she told me that kids on the playground were calling her a crybaby. Just then I had a wave of insight wash over me. I found a safe place to pull over. I told her I was sorry she had to deal with mean kids. I also went on to tell her that being sensitive wasn't all bad. She screamed, "I HATE IT!" I let her have her moment. Then I asked her what was wrong with being sensitive and having a huge heart? What was wrong with wanting to understand and get things right or helping someone else when they are having a hard time? She said nothing. I said, "Maybe, just maybe, you can look at your sensitivity in a new way." She sat up a bit higher and asked, "What way?" I told her she might not know it but having a heart and being sensitive was her gift. I went on to tell her that her only job was learning how to manage all her emotions and overwhelming feelings when they came up. So when she started feeling those tears well up, she should take a deep breath and be patient with herself. I could tell it pleased her deeply to know she wasn't a crybaby, that her heart was her gift. At that moment I realized what Jenna needed most. She needed me.

Pirates of the Caribbean

When we added a deck to our home Luke and Jenna loved spraying it down with the hose while Luke would prop the broom or squeegee and push the water off. Something about this process and the boards of the deck made them imagine the deck was a pirate ship. I tell this story because it was such a joy for me to watch Jenna interact with Luke. Before she started spraying she would always make sure Luke had the tool he wanted to use all propped up and ready. Nine times out of ten she would let Luke lead the pretend scenario they were playing out. Many times I was taken prisoner until they would get hungry. Being raised alongside Luke, Jenna was able to develop her gift of being sensitive and showing her heart.

Tinkerbelle Café

I don't think there is a kid out there who doesn't love playing with cardboard boxes. Jenna is no different. Her box creation that stands out the most to me and really shows her creativity and heart is from when we got a new refrigerator. She decided to make a house that served tea. This was how the Tinkerbelle Café was born. She decorated the outside while Glen cut a hole out so she could serve "real" hot tea out the window. I asked her who her customers would be. She said, "Grandma!" We even have a picture of her serving tea to her grandma out the window of the Tinkerbell Café.

It Stresses Me Out!

Up until this conversation I had with Jenna, I had always brought her with me and Luke to his doctor appointments. She was young and it was just easier to bring her along instead of trying to find a sitter. However, as she got older, I had been thinking about stopping this practice as muscular dystrophy was ravaging Luke's body further. I knew the talk would be heavy and I knew it would be emotionally tough for me. I felt she just didn't need to hear how bad Luke was getting. Little did I know she was already thinking the very same thing. She actually told me she was relieved because in her words, "IT STRESSES ME OUT!" It was incredible to hear her be so aware of herself and her feelings. It was real growth on her part. I did have feelings of brief guilt that I hadn't seen it before, but boy did it feel good to start seeing progress in Jenna handling her feelings. And she even expressed them in a truthful manner.

The Heart in My Pocket

I am not 100% positive when Jenna found her first heart shaped rock, but I do remember when she gave me my first one. I was standing in security at the airport emptying my pockets because the alarm kept beeping and they wouldn't let me through. I was taking everything out of my pockets and there amongst the coins and one lone earring was a very little heart shaped rock. I was touched so deeply as it was a sign that she was getting from me what she needed. Further, I was delighted that she was showing her love for me.

Glasses

I asked Jenna why she was squinting at the TV and she said it was because she couldn't see it well. What? How long had this been going on? She wasn't sure... a long time. I couldn't believe it. Here she was after being held back to take 2nd grade over again and it turns out she can't see? It was like, duh! Sure enough, she needed glasses. At first she hated the idea. She cried to me, "But Mom, I'll look stupid." I told her to look at me. I said, "I'm your mom and the last thing I'll let happen is for you to look stupid. I bet we find really pretty glasses to bring out the green in your eyes!" And we did. She has now tried contacts but always goes back to glasses. Somehow I had to make sure she started realizing that she mattered just as much as Luke.

Peace Teacher

With Jenna as sensitive as she was, I knew her 4th grade teacher needed to be caring but firm, creative but structured enough that Jenna felt supported. It was especially important since Jenna had already been held back and had an Individual Education Plan. Besides having a brother like Luke, she already felt so different and her emotions still often threatened to overwhelm her. This meant her new teacher also needed to be mindful of her issues, without letting Jenna get away with feeling sorry for herself. I was hoping another adult could help Jenna learn new ways of coping, but I was almost certain this was wishful thinking. I went to all the 4th grade teachers' rooms and talked to a few of them. The last classroom I walked into was empty, as the teacher wasn't there yet. I looked around and saw peace signs from all over the world. There was a tree with no leaves but with blown eggs hanging from the branches, and collected rocks lying around here and there. There were newspaper articles tacked up about animals. Whoever this teacher was, I knew she was truly caring, knowledgeable and loved life, just like my Jenna. I instantly knew this was the right teacher for Jenna. Mrs. Jones ended up being the best medicine we could have hoped for. Jenna was lucky enough to have her for 5th grade as well. Even to this day, Mrs. Jones is a support person not only for Jenna but for our entire family. She taught Jenna the very useful technique of taking a moment to collect herself whenever she felt the emotions well up inside her. I see Jenna using this technique often. It makes me so proud she isn't stuffing her feelings down but rather letting them wash through her as needed. I need to internalize that lesson as well.

No More Bread

The final factor in Jenna's outbursts revealed its ugly head when I had to start picking her up from school because her tummy hurt. We started noticing a bad smell to her breath, and big circles under her eyes. Many nights I'd find her lying on the bathroom floor bloated and miserable. Plus her emotions were in full swing. But the worst thing I noticed was that she was losing weight she didn't have to lose. We had already taken her off dairy so I knew this wasn't her issue. Everything I read about Jenna's symptoms pointed to gluten intolerance. I had been experiencing some symptoms as well so we went off gluten together and we scheduled a doctor's appointment for Jenna in 4 days' time. By the second day off gluten her symptoms were completely gone and I was starting to feel much better as well. We tested her for celiac's disease, which thankfully was negative, and scheduled another appointment for a month down the road. Jenna ended up gaining back 7 pounds in 30 days. And I lost 2 inches from around my waist! It was a challenge going gluten free but we managed, and now we have fun trying new recipes or remaking the really good ones we find.

Chapter Three: Love Rocks

"Only from your heart can you touch the sky." ~ Rumi

By this point in Jenna's life Luke was a senior in High School and Jenna was in 5th grade. There was this feeling of, he made it. He had made it longer then we were told he would. My Jenna was happy, her grades were coming up. Then Luke got severely sick. We were flung back in the trenches of a great amount of fear, sleep loss, and insurmountable stress. This was one of the scariest blips of time I had ever experienced. It must have been for Jenna too.

Don't Die Without Me

After the Homecoming dance in October 2009, Luke and 300 other students ended up with the swine flu. But since Luke had Duchenne on top of the swine flu, he ended up with pneumonia. So off to the hospital we went; I was pretty sure he would be admitted. We were all scared, knowing this could take Luke's life. I thought we had managed not to alarm Jenna as she seemed to get up and go to school just fine. She appeared to be rolling with the punches. As we were loading the van up to take Luke to the hospital the phone rang and it was Jenna leaving a message. She was crying, telling me to tell Luke, "Don't die without me!" I called her back and told her if things got worse I'd send for her. I promised!

In Your Face Duchenne Muscular Dystrophy, All Pain, All GLORY!

If you've read my book In Your Face you know Luke made a full recovery and it was this event that inspired me to write it in the first place. I wanted to capture his life's essence while he was still here with me. Little did I know what impact this book about Luke's life would have on the world of Duchenne or even how much of an impression it would make on Jenna, even though she had been in the face of Duchenne Muscular Dystrophy the entire time.

She Got Her Hug

During the editing and final writing of In Your Face I learned about a new electrical stimulation of the nerve treatment called the STS that was already helping boys with Duchenne. When I shared this news with Jenna, including a video of a boy getting stronger, she looked at me and asked, "You mean Luke could hug me back?" I just squeezed her and said, "We will see, I sure hope so!" We knew the treatment wasn't a cure but we were hopeful for any positive results. On the third day of treatment Luke had regained some strength and mobility. He cried to us that he had thought he'd never get to feel good again. And yes, Jenna did get her hug as the photo shows at the beginning of this chapter.

Victory Bible Camp

When Luke headed to MDA summer camp each summer, Jenna would go to Victory Bible Camp. She always had such great fun with the water sports, craft activities, food, worship songs, and campfires. The summer of 2010 was no different; we had just gotten back from Luke's Texas trip where she got her hug. She was feeling on top of the world. We all were. When her week was finished at camp and I picked her up, she had a big white cross painted on one cheek. She told me it was for Luke.

Mom, Look!

I went running into her room thinking it was an emergency! When I got in there she was standing with her left leg out holding her pajama bottom up. I was like, WHAT? She was like, LOOK! Still I was clueless, and I could tell by the look she gave me that she thought so too. She had always had this small, pea-sized, light red blotch of a birthmark on her leg. But, suddenly and beautifully, it had transformed into the shape of a heart! Her entire being radiated delight in her new finding. I thought, how perfectly fitting for my girl with a HUGE heart.

Chapter Four: Big Hearted

"A kind heart is a fountain of gladness, making everything in its vicinity freshen into smiles." ~ Washington Irving

Jenna not only finds heart shaped rocks, she's an expert in finding hearts in nature everywhere she goes.

We have heart shaped rocks in every windowsill, in cup holders and pockets, in my purse and on my desk. Jenna gives them to people she cares about all the time. It's her way of saying, "My heart sees the heart in you, and I care." What's so beautiful to see in her is that through all of Luke's surgeries, his life struggle to live with his disease, and all the turmoil she has witnessed the family go through, she has found her own way of being happy. She remains full of love, willing to share it at the drop of a hat. She gives her heart gently, but full on.

She has told me that finding heart shaped rocks is like finding signs that everything is going to be okay.

Lego Nation

Jenna's dad, Glen, built what we referred to as the Big Table. Basically it was a counter top with four legs, tall enough that Luke could park his wheelchair and prop his hands up on the edge so he and Jenna could play games, before his hands got too weak to build Legos together. Before the STS treatment, which is now called the Vecttor, Jenna did most of the building while Luke directed her. They would spend hours building contraptions and playing games together. One day I had run to the store and when I came back, Luke and Jenna were beaming with pride. Jenna said, "His hands are getting stronger!" Luke said, "I built this truck all by myself without assistance from Jenna." This was the beginning of what ended up being Lego Nation filling up half of our living room. When Luke moved out the first time we had to pack up all the buildings, Lego trucks and people so we could put them in our basement. Jenna delicately put each piece into its own labeled bag and carefully placed all the sets together in boxes, also labeled. The idea was for them to build them all back downstairs.

Gold Mine Conversation

Luke moving out was hard on us all, but it was probably the hardest on me. I experienced empty-nest syndrome coupled with the fact that I was scared out of my mind I'd lose him while he was gone. I hadn't ever really thought he'd move out completely. On one hand, I was thrilled for him, but I knew that things could change in a heartbeat. One of the things that Glen, Jenna, and I did without Luke was to travel to a gold mine in the heart of the Alaskan wilderness. It was a trip that wouldn't be possible for Luke to take with us, but he had moved out and his care was covered. During this trip Jenna and I were walking back to camp when I told her, "I miss Luke." She replied, "I do too." I went on and said, "For the first time Luke feels he can live." She said, "I know." Then I told her how I wanted to be the best mom, the best wife, and to write more books. Jenna stopped and looked at me. She said, "Just one problem with that. You already are the best mom."

"Was I wanted?"

It seems that Jenna and I have most of our conversations in the car, either on the way to school or after. And this day was no different. She asked me, "Was I wanted?" I responded immediately, "Yes, you were the best surprise ever!" She said, "Surprise?" I said, "Yes, you were wanted, you just weren't planned." I went on to tell her that she is meant to be here in every sense of the word. Her life means something very special and she is my angel. She knew what I meant since I had almost died giving birth to her.

Middle School Blossom

When Jenna started middle school, I was scared for her. I know how kids can behave toward other kids, and with her being so sensitive I could only imagine Jenna's heart being stepped on all the time. She's had some challenges but overall it's been a delight to see her grow. All her teachers tell me what a joy it is to have her in the school. They say that her caring and compassion are generous. They also love how dedicated she is to doing her class work to the best of her abilities. I notice she often helps those kids that need some extra help. Yes, she has a heart but in no way is she weak. Her spirit is strong and full of grace. She is truly a living example of how we all need to live.

Orange Crush

Luke had moved out and was trying to live his life with more independence. I didn't know how long this would last for him so I decided that Jenna and I needed a quality mother-daughter trip to Maui. We met up with family there but before we did, we were picking up our small economy car from the car rental when they said we had earned a "free" upgrade to a Jeep with a removable roof. Jenna's eyes got big, she started jumping up and down saying "Can we, can we?!" So of course we ended up driving away in a little orange Jeep she named Orange Crush. We toured around Maui and drove the Hana Highway. We had a ball. It was a time we will never forget. We took numerous pictures of ourselves hanging out the top of Orange Crush. We even found matching Orange Crush T-shirts.

Home Again

When Luke moved back home as an adult, it rocked the boat a bit for Jenna since she had been used to getting all the attention for six months by this point. However, she loved having him back home. Finally there was a brother to talk to again, to play games with again. She would watch Luke play his favorite PlayStation games for hours. She also liked that he could help her with her homework. This time was highly stressful since his health had been compromised further by Duchenne, but we also had times of great fun. We started doing what we called Fiesta Friday every weekend. I would make tacos, and Luke would break out the music which he insisted made my food taste better. We would dance, play, and laugh as a family. We all loved Friday.

Her Babies

With Jenna's and my gluten sensitivity, I cook with a lot of eggs, and since Jenna loves animals so much, we decided to get some laying hens. When the babies (as she referred to them) arrived, she was over the moon. She took pictures of them all and gave them all egg names. There were Eggy, Sunny, Scrambles, and the favorite, Shelly. Sadly, Shelly didn't make it. When Jenna saw Shelly not moving she cried and cried. Later in the season, after they had all started laying eggs, our new favorite was Sunny. When you came in the coop she'd greet you with a peep and stretch her neck in saying hello. She'd climb up in Jenna's hand and sit. It was so adorable. And then we lost Sunny on Christmas Eve. Again, Jenna cried and cried.

13th Birthday

None of us could believe Jenna was becoming a teenager. The theme she chose was a hippie peace sign birthday party. We had so much fun. One of the things Jenna does before she opens each gift is to read out loud each birthday card. Before she could read well, she made me do it. I've always found this so endearing. It really shows how much she cares about people and how she likes to make everyone feel good. This time, the card that choked her (and everyone) up was the card from Luke.

To my sister, who knows me – who I am, what I think, how I feel, and loves me inside and out…

Who laughs me out of my too serious moments, talks me through the ones that really matter, and stands by my side all the way…

My sister whose heart is so warm, whose caring means so much, who's loved in so many ways…

Happy Birthday to my really special sister.

Love, Luke

Walks with Luke

From the time Jenna was born, Luke and I would take walks with her. As she grew and he ended up in his wheelchair full time this practice didn't change. When she was small she'd ride on the back of his wheelchair. She loved being with him. As they grew up, the walks evolved into time they'd spend taking pictures of our beautiful Alaskan mountains, animals, and scenery. They'd spend hours outside pretending and just being brother and sister. I loved watching them outside together, seemingly without a stress in the world.

Love at First Sight

Out of the eleven pups left none of them seemed just right for my Jenna. They were all cute, as puppies are, but we didn't see "the one." I could tell that many of them would be real handfuls to raise properly, and I wanted a dog that Jenna could handle well. We were about to leave when I saw a smaller pup, probably the runt of the litter, buried in a blanket and fast asleep. I asked the owner if we could see her. She said, "Sure, but this one is the runt." As she picked her up to hand her to Jenna, Jenna immediately lifted the pup to look at her, and the pup opened her eyes and sniffed Jenna's nose. Jenna's look said it all. It was love at first sight for both Jenna and her new puppy, Josie.

Chapter Five: The Heart Within

"The heart that truly loves, never forgets."

Luke had moved out and moved back in and then moved into his very own home within one year. A lot of things happened in a very short period of time, and six months after Luke moved into his own home, his untimely death hit us out of nowhere. Duchenne had weakened his body to the point where he couldn't fight any more.

Living on his own was an accomplishment we all played an important role in. Jenna was a huge help to her brother and looked forward to the time she got to spend with him in his new home.

Keeping House

When Luke moved back, his plan was to find a place of his own that we'd help him manage his life from. It was very important for him to have as much independence as he possibly could. On move-in day Jenna was so excited for him. She helped him decorate and set it all up. Once it was all set up she went over on Sunday afternoons for game day. Then I'd bring dinner and we'd all eat together.

Beach Dream

"Mom, did I tell you about my beach dream I had the other night?" I said no. "Well, Luke and I were at the beach and it was almost dark. The stars had just starting coming out when Luke got up and started walking toward a light. He turned back towards me and smiled and walked into the light." Then she said, "I was so happy for him." When she was telling me the dream it occurred to me that it might be a premonition, but I pushed that thought swiftly from my mind. I focused on listening to her. She told me she took the dream as a sign that everything was going to be okay.

Cloudy Cold Day

As Luke was lying in the hospital taking his last breaths of life, the minutes rolled into hours. It was a bitter cold dreary day with the clouds rolling in, covering Luke's mountains that we could see from his 2nd floor room. Jenna would come into the room for a few minutes, then leave again, unreadable without saying anything. I was so worried for my family, for myself. Would Luke pull out of this? I thought not. On one of her trips into the room I said to Luke that his room had a great view but that clouds had covered his mountains. This must have made an impression on Jenna because the next time she came in the room, she taped up a picture she had drawn on lined paper of the sun coming out over the mountains. She had written underneath. "I BROUGHT YOU YOUR MOUNTAINS BACK. Love, Jenna."

For My Brother

We all wanted to put something special in Luke's casket to be buried with him. We all gathered individual items that we wanted. The first thing Jenna added was all the "gotcha rocks" we'd gathered over the years. Gotcha rocks were the little rocks Luke's wheelchair brought into the house that we stepped on. He would always say "Gotcha!" when we did. Then Jenna went to her room and found the most perfect heart shaped rock to go with him.

Epilogue: Living Life through Jenna-Colored Glasses

One day not long ago, I was telling Jenna how neat it was for her to be achieving the good grades she has been getting and how well she seems to be doing, especially since grieving her brother hasn't been easy. She told me, "It's probably because I'm not worried anymore. I miss him, but I am not worried."

We have heart shaped rocks in every windowsill, in cup holders and pockets, in my purse and on my desk. Jenna gives them to people she cares about all the time. It is her way of saying, "My heart sees the heart in you, and I care." What's incredibly beautiful for me to witness about Jenna is that through all of Luke's surgeries, his life struggle living a disease, his death, all the grief, and the crazy turmoil she has witnessed and gone through personally, she has found her own way of being happy and full of love, and she is willing to share it at the drop of a hat. She gives her heart gently, but full on.

"If she's crying, don't say anything. Just hug her."

On any given day, no matter the season, you can send Jenna out to find a heart shaped rock and she'll come back more times than not with more than one. She has told me that finding heart shaped rocks is like finding signs that everything is going to be okay. They are there just for her to find.

Jenna's Heart Shaped Rock Finding Recipe:

"Let go of it having to be a perfect shaped heart, because rocks are like people. We are all different and none of us are perfect."

Thrive Through Tears; anyway

This is the rest of the story just before, during, and after Luke's passing. I tell it to share how his death has impacted me in both ways you can imagine and ways that have left me with the understanding that the connections we have with our children last for eternity. Get ready for a tissue-grabbing unconventional ride.

Something Was Off

Luke had been suffering from what he said was his stomach hurting after he ate. We brought it up to the doctor who said if it didn't clear up soon, Luke could have his GI tract checked. Luke didn't like this idea. He was always cautious since he'd already had several surgeries, and he was adamant about not having holes in his body other than the ones he was born with. This meant no tracheotomy holes in his neck to assist his breathing, and no food tube holes other than his mouth.

A couple of weeks before Luke's colon twisted, Luke told me he was afraid of not having his own say over his life. I understood, and I promised him I would make sure he got his say even if I didn't agree. I didn't know when I made that promise that I'd be tested on it so quickly and so finally.

It was Saturday and all day I kept worrying about Luke. I had this nagging feeling that something was wrong. I talked to him by phone, we texted, but I still couldn't shake the feeling. My husband and I were out shopping and we had gone a different way than we normally do when I noticed a building that seemed very out of place against the Alaska mountain sky. I even commented on it to Glen, "Doesn't that building look like it belongs in Arizona or Mexico?"

A little while later I went over to Luke's house to drop off a movie. When I kissed him on the forehead he felt clammy. He said he was fine. I wasn't home for more than 30 minutes when his care provider called to tell me to get over there, that Luke was turning blue and the paramedics were on the way. I kept yelling over and over to my husband, "I knew it, I knew something was wrong!"

Going into Luke's house was a scene I wasn't entirely prepared for. It was a scene I'd rather not relive but that I must share. Luke's body was rigid in pain and he was blue, he could barely breathe. He kept asking me if he was going to be okay. I told him he was and that the ambulance was on the way.

"Are you ready to go to heaven?"

Sitting there listening to the doctor tell Luke he needed to have his colon removed and Luke refusing wasn't surprising. By this point Luke was in so much pain he was only moving his head to communicate his yes or no answers. All his answers were no except one. As I write this tears stream down my face. It was and still is something I'll never forget as long as I live. The doctor asked Luke, "Are you ready to go to heaven?" Luke knew I was right there, he hesitated and started to cry while nodding his head yes. My mind was screaming… WHAT??? I couldn't believe it. All I could do was cry. I asked Luke if he wanted to go back to his house, but he shook his head no.

They Lined the Halls

The hospital staff was amazing. As more and more friends and family came and lined both sides of the hall, they opened another hospital room. They brought in snacks. I still had hope that somehow,

Luke's colon would fix itself. However, Luke's body started to go into sepsis by the end of the next day. I knew it wouldn't be long.

Wait for Me

It was 2 a.m. when I awoke with a start. I glanced over at Luke. There was a change in his breathing. I knew it was almost time. I whisper-cried to him to wait for me, that I needed to leave the room but that I'd be back. "Please wait for me." He didn't disappoint. I came back and nestled into the makeshift bed I had made next to him and held onto his hand as I watched the pulse slowly fade from his neck. The look on his face was one of total GLORY and AWE as if to tell me, "Mom, you are not going to believe this." I know whatever he was seeing was an amazing beautiful sight. He looked like an angel. The entire room changed in an instant. He was gone. I told him, in a matter of fact way, "I will see you again. I will be okay."

Lock of Hair

It was time to say goodbye. But first I had to pick out the mortuary to send Luke's body to. I just picked the first one on the page. I thought, does it really matter?

After this the nurses asked me if I wanted to wash Luke's body and if I needed any help. I said yes, but what I really needed to have was a lock of his hair. I couldn't bring myself to do it, but the lovely nurse helped me. The worst was yet to happen though.

Watching strangers take your child's body away is like someone trying to rip out your very soul. I've never heard a sound so primal as the one that came out of me. The word agony doesn't even come close to what I was feeling.

Driving Home

Climbing into the truck with Luke's belongings, knowing he wasn't coming with us was numbing. I felt so empty inside. The only thing breaking through was the cold of the 15 below zero weather we were having. It chilled me to the bone. All I could think was that I'd never get to write that book with Luke that he wanted to write.

Glen, Jenna, and I were lost, hurt and in shock. We were each quiet in our own mental loop of pain. How were we supposed to pick up the pieces? We all had known this day would come but did it have to happen so soon? We wanted more time.

The next day it was time to go to the mortuary. I had no idea, but the mortuary I picked was in the same building I had commented on that Saturday, just hours before Luke's emergency. It was surreal, walking into this weird, out-of-place building to pick out my son's casket. Then we went on to the florist. It seemed like a cruel joke or a bad dream I would surely wake up from at any moment. Finally we went to pick out his resting place at the graveyard. We found the perfect place: it was overlooked by Luke's beloved mountain, Pioneer Peak, and the number of the plot was 3, the number of Dale Earnhardt Senior, who was Luke's all-time favorite Nascar driver. It was perfect.

Let Others Take Care of You

I wracked my grief-stricken numb brain trying to come up with something to say for Luke's Celebration of Life. I did eventually write it out. I was planning to speak, but the morning of the funeral, in the shower, the words "let others take care of you" kept running through my mind. I shared this with my sister. She said not to worry about it. Although there are times I wish I had spoken, my sister was able to get up and share exactly what I wanted to have said. It was perfect. Especially the part about Luke being a rebel.

Non Essential Angels

I was a crazy person. I remembered that over Christmas, a little store called Non Essentials had these beautiful handmade aluminum angels in their window display. I decided I HAD to have one. When I drove up to the store, I noticed there were none in the window. I was disheartened but decided to wait outside until they opened. The owner met me at the door telling me how sorry she was to hear about Luke and asking how she could help me. When I explained what I wanted, she told me she was sold out. But then she said if I could wait a minute she'd have her son bring a couple to choose from her own collection. I told her no, that it was okay. She gently took my arm and said she really wanted me to have one. So I waited. She ended up giving them both to me free of charge. One of the angels was actually a candle holder.

Cards, Flowers, Gifts

Everyone has been incredibly good to me. I will treasure each card, every flower and every gift that was sent to me. I will hold them dear always. Luke's grandpa made a memento box for it all. The angels are displayed around my house and on Luke's altar. His altar is located where he always sat during meal times. His pictures grace the walls of our home. One Christmas Luke gave me a large picture frame to fill with photos that reads: memories and happy moments live in our hearts forever. Those words ring so very true.

500 Candles

Luke's name means the bearer of light. So for me, lighting candles wasn't just something that made me feel better, but also a way for me to pay my respects to a person, my son. Someone who gave me, well, me.

During the first year after his death I burned over 500 candles. I kept one of those religious candles burning day and night, but I also burned hundreds of tea lights and votive candles as well.

On Luke's birthday I took the 60+ empty religious candle holders over to his resting place and lit them all. We had family and friends go and light candles in his honor as well.

You could see the glow of all the candles from the road. It was so beautiful.

Luke's Place

A few days after Luke's service, after everyone had left, I went to Luke's house. We called it "Luke's Place".

Outside his door, a dear friend of mine had placed a four foot lighted angel blowing on a horn. The tears were flowing freely from my eyes now.

Walking through the door it seemed like we had just finally gotten him settled in. Everything still smelled new. His weekend care provider had just mopped, his laundry was all done, his fridge was still full of groceries he had purchased. His fish were still fluttering in his tank. So I fed them.

I knew it would soon be time to move Luke's stuff out. I gave myself a month. As he had lived just up the road from us, it made the move something I could do little by little. I was so grateful the landlords had given me all the time I needed to empty his house out. It was something I needed to do by myself. It was the final time I could take care of my boy.

The Year of Firsts

The first year of Luke's passing was the worst by far, and in many ways it was a complete blur. I think I cried five lifetimes of tears. I cried so much I wondered where all the water came from.

It started with our first wedding anniversary without him, then my birthday, Valentine's Day and Easter. Mother's Day was the worst, then my first summer, his favorite season, without him. 4th of July, then Thanksgiving, HIS BIRTHDAY, Christmas, New Year's, not to mention his first angelversary in heaven! None of it was fun, but I got through it with help from family and friends, and burning over 500 candles in 12 months. I did manage, even when I thought I was going crazy from my mother's grief, to publish *Heart Shaped Rocks* and an eBook called *Luke's Light, A Vision of Hope*, which is a book of Luke's poetry.

During that year of firsts I read everything I could get my hands on about grief. It also brought on an unquenchable thirst to know what happens to us when we die. I NEEDED to know what that look on Luke's face meant. I NEEDED to make sure I would see him again. I started reading about near death experiences, over 20 titles. I started with *Heaven is for Real*, *Waking up in Heaven* and *Proof of Heaven* to name a few. I still read books on this topic as I come across them.

I believe in God as my higher power but I know there is more to the story. I got a tattoo in memory of Luke, his life, and his passing that says "Through Him You Shall Know Me". I went to church every Sunday after Luke passed for several months. I could feel him there. I remember actually having the sensation of his arm around me. Despite my faith, I have a hard time with the whole "we are sinners" thing and I struggle with the idea that there is only one way to get to heaven. I believe God is infinitely better than that. Our true nature, even if we've forgotten, is the same... total and complete LOVE.

The year of firsts taught me that Grief is an irrational beast. It is normal, natural, and completely necessary. As Eckhart Tolle said, "When death is denied, life loses its depth." Meaning, don't try to shortchange the grief journey by not *feeling* your grief. Love will see you through.

Letters to Luke

I've said many times that Luke wasn't just my son; he was also my friend, my confidant, and my cheerleader. My role as Luke's caregiver created a space for us to be open with our feelings. Whether we were angry, happy, mad, sad, glad or frustrated, we were together as partners in crime and yes, as soul mates, getting through the ravages of life-threatening, debilitating disease. We would laugh, tell jokes, and even rage at each other. Whatever the emotion, we shared it with one another. Now, not having him around physically is a huge challenge. So I started a *Letters to Luke* journal. It is a way for me to keep my connection with him. Through these letters I talk with him, I reflect, and I ask questions, mostly so that he can help me be a better me. And boy, does he answer.

Little Bird

In my quest to learn more about grief and death, I landed on a Facebook page called *Angels at my Door*, which led me to their website. I then read the free eBook *Love you Forever*, which documented experiences of people connecting through a medium to their loved ones that had passed. The next thing I knew I was setting up an appointment for an over-the-phone reading. That appointment turned out to be one of the best things I had done since Luke passed. It gave me such comfort to have a woman who had never met me or my family recount intimate details about us and Luke, stuff that nobody knows about but me. It's really a gift that keeps on giving. She told me many things that absolutely resonated with me. She shared how Luke will come through just for me with certain signs.. Like boom, boom, boom. She told me that Luke showed her how I told him in a matter of fact way, "I will see you again."

The one thing she told me that I really want to share has to do with my daughter, Jenna. A new store had opened about thirty minutes from where we live. Jenna had gotten really good grades so I thought we'd go in there and find something special for her. We looked and looked until she finally came upon a bird necklace that said HOPE on it. She had tears in her eyes when she showed me and told me it reminded her of Luke. I agreed it was the perfect something special we were looking for. Mainly because up until this point, school had been challenging for Jenna and she attributed the improved grades to the fact that she no longer has to worry about Luke anymore. Luke always called her J bird since the name Jenna means "little bird."

As the reading went on, Luke came through with a message. The medium asked if there was any shop or little store where we live that had a boardwalk on front of it. At first I said no, why? She said that Luke showed her a store front, then a bird. She said, "This doesn't make sense to me, does it make sense to you?" Through tears in my eyes I told her that I understood the bird part. Then I said, "Wait..." That store not only has a boardwalk in the front, but Boardwalk is actually the name of the store!

Luke's main message for me is that he is surrounding me with violet purple and blue healing light to give me energy. This is why the cover of this book was designed the way it is.

Grief Isn't a Part of My Personality

It's true. I'm a fun-loving, naturally optimistic person who completely believes that life challenges are meant to make us stronger. Grief just doesn't fit in with how I want to live my life. I know when we experience loss we will always grieve, but I want to thrive through tears anyway.

The worst kind of grief is your own grief, to be sure. Grief feels so foreign in the beginning, and you struggle to find your footing. But there comes a point where you must desire healing, or fall victim to the pain.

"Grief never ends… But it changes.

It's a passage, not a place to stay.

Grief is not a sign of weakness, nor a lack of faith.

It is the price of love."

~Author Unknown

Unbreakable Connection

I've asked for signs and talked to God for as long as I can remember. So it seemed natural for me to start asking Luke to help guide me. I'm always talking to him or writing him letters. Not long after he passed, I was asked if I wanted to do a guided meditation to help me release the pain of my mother's grief. At first, I wanted to refuse. It seemed that grief was all I had left. It's what seemed humanly real and I wasn't too sure I liked the sound of releasing my grief. It sort of sounded like I'd be releasing Luke all over again. It was not something I was even remotely interested in. But I said sure and we scheduled my guided meditation to be done over Skype. I almost canceled several times, which ultimately made me even more curious.

When the time came, I was immediately drawn into the meditation as she described my front yard, the fire, the tall trees. She also described what kind of night it was: dark, stars shining with the moon. It was quite lovely. Now, mind you, I had never met this woman before in my life and she lives in the UK and I in Alaska. Yet even the music she used resonated with me. It was crazy, but very grounding and soothing.

One particular part about the unbreakable cord, the connection that Luke and I will always have, left me feeling very much at peace. She sent me the recording which I revisit a couple times a week. Sometimes I go awhile without feeling the need to connect with Luke in this way. But I get something new out of it every time. It's been so helpful that I will be offering this kind of meditation on my website to help other grieving mothers.

"Mom it's okay, I'm right here, you got this."

I hope this next story I share with you is as enlightening as it is inspirational.

Recently I learned how rituals can help clear unwanted memories and feelings. I have now done them numerous times, so I know how effective they can be.

There were three days that Luke was on his death bed, starting when his colon twisted, continuing to the ambulance ride, and then at the hospital where his heart beat for the last time. This time period, culminating in his body finally being taken away, was something I was having a really hard time with. Every time I hear an ambulance or see one, I'm sent right back to that time. I try to shake it, but it leaves me panicky. I try to think, "It's okay Misty, they are helping someone else get the proper care." Nothing works. To make matters worse, the ambulances in our town are kept one road over from where I live. So this happens as much as a few times a week, sometimes even daily.

I decided to design a ritual around this entire ordeal. I found one of those fire starter logs that burns for three hours. For me, three hours represents those three days that Luke was on his death bed. Then I wrote all the horrible memories I wanted to clear on notecards to burn. My plan was to drive the same route the ambulance had taken, then go to my fire pit to have the ritual ceremony.

On the night I decided would work the best, since both my husband and daughter wouldn't be home, I kept trying to talk myself out of it. I dropped my daughter off and all the way home, I thought of reason after reason why I shouldn't go through with it. Luke had lived just up the road from us, not even half a mile away. I was talking to Luke, getting ready to turn left, but I had to wait for what looked like a truck from a distance. It was dark so I wasn't sure. All I knew is it was going super slow. UGH, I was just going to go home, maybe I would do this dumb ritual another time. As the truck approached I saw that it wasn't a truck but indeed an ambulance! And it was actually the very same ambulance! Tears came instantly to my eyes. As the ambulance passed I could feel Luke saying, "Mom it's okay, I'm right here, you got this." I knew I had to go through with the ritual after all.

As I got out of my truck to retrieve the log and the notecards to burn, I realized the night was the exact same night that was described to me in my guided mediation!

I was tested like crazy after this ritual to see if it was really clear. I saw an ambulance coming up from behind me, lights and sirens blaring, code red. And yes, it was the same ambulance again. I ended up right behind it. It turned down the road I live on! Then it turned again just before the road to Luke's. I didn't feel panicky, not one bit. I went home as usual, curious who needed the ambulance in such a rush and sending up a prayer that all would be well. All I felt was amusement, as there was no residual emotion to deal with.

Luke Days

Luke Days are the sunny days you might hear about in a country song. No matter the season, Luke loved them all. Especially summer. These are the days we even take the "Luke way" home. A scenic mountainous view – the long way around.

Sometimes we hop on his buggy and get a little mud on the tires. Sometimes we even roll the windows down and cruise.

Embracing Mother's Grief

The cord of connection between a mother and child looks delicate and fragile, yet it is immensely strong and can never be broken.

You go from loving in the present to loving in the absent. My mother's grief is now a part of who I am. It will be with me as long as I grace this planet, until I see my beautiful, amazing son again. It is a journey of unknown length of time.

I am humbled to the core in my mother's grief. I will use all that I've learned and continue to learn, all my life lessons, through my mistakes, my human ignorance and selfishness, to assist, love, and support others. I will try to lead by example by being the best me.

Instead of wallowing in the pain and sadness, instead of living in the why did this happen to my son, or thinking about the marriage he will never have, or all the milestones of life he isn't going to meet, or the excruciating feeling that I will have to miss watching him do it all... I choose to live in the continuance of our unbreakable connection.

I choose to thrive through tears anyway.

I'm doing it

Losing a child takes you to the lowest of lows, through the depths of unimaginable sadness and the depression-like state of loss. The emotional, spiritual, and physical strain from this magnitude of grief creates stress on the body. This stress can include many symptoms and can lead to your immune system being compromised. Within six months to a year after the loss, many people will have a health crisis of their own to deal with. No person can keep that much pain inside without it escaping in some way.

Mine showed up in my gallbladder. During my son's passing and the days that followed I remember hunching over and hugging myself around my middle. It also seemed I would need to take a deep breath several times in just one hour. Then there were the times I felt I would explode, thinking I was going crazy, or getting all panicky with anxiety. Never before had pain been so loud. I figured that carrying it around was something I would just have to get used to, that it was something I'd somehow learn to live with. However with focused intent, we can heal even in grief. We can even come out the other side stronger than before.

I know this because I'm doing it and I believe my role is to assist other parents who've lost children to do the same. I've been taught by the best to release the pain of grief on a regular basis, I've learned how to keep my connection with my child alive and to use all natural strategies to balance my body systems so that I can be a more healthy and vibrant me. These are tools and rituals I wished I had known about years ago.

According to Aurora Winter from the Grief Coach Academy, it takes the average person 5-8 years to get through the grief process. It is a process that doesn't need to last this long. Anyone can learn.

Love Story within a Love Story

Once upon a time there was a little boy who struggled every day to simply walk, at the time he was too young to have the concept his body was actually fighting to stay alive. One day he brought home the most spindly looking flower for his mother. The flower happened to be a dahlia which he knew held a special place in her heart. When his mother learned that the dahlia grows tubers you can divide to have more dahlia plants every year, she knew she had to plant them. She thought what better way to have something from her son for the years when his physical presence was no longer. When the day came for this to be true she planted them in his honor, to her surprise with each bloom came healing. It was like her son loving her from heaven. And to her dismay the birth of something new, her very own flower farm, All Dahlia'd Up.

The gift of this love story within a love story is her son's life and death has shown her that anyone can thrive and bloom no matter what happens.

Who is Misty VanderWeele

Misty is a flower farmer, author, child loss grief survivor, and speaker.

Before her son's passing, Misty was mostly known for her advocacy work and books about Duchenne Muscular Dystrophy. She got her first pair of grief wings after her dad died when she was 19 years old. In the following years she lost all her grandparents, three aunts, and then a cousin to suicide in 2014. Despite previous loss, her son's passing riveted her to the core and had her seeking signs from him, and fueling her desire to know more about what happens to us when we die. She intuitively knew she had learn ways to cope and mostly that she didn't want to live in a constant state of pain and sadness and that ultimately it was up to her in how she lived the rest of her life. *Thrive Through Tears; anyway* is how she is doing just that.

Misty currently lives in Palmer, Alaska on a large vegetable farm surrounded by fields and the great Alaskan Mountains with her daughter, Jenna, and her husband, Glen. In the summer you can add vibrant dahlia flowers of many different vibrant colors to the mix.

You can find her online at:
Facebook: www.Facebook.com/MistyVanderweele
Instagram @All_Dahliad_Up
Pinterest: AllDahliadUp
Website: www.MistyVanderweele.com

All Dahlia'd Up Flower Farm

AllDahliadUp.com

To Bloom & Share the Miracle & Vibrancy of Life One Flower at a Time

Like **Thrive Through Tears Anyway?**
Then you'll <u>LOVE</u> **Thrive *it* UP**

Available on KINDLE

amazon

90 Original Quotes to Thrive not Just Survive

www.ingramcontent.com/pod-product-compliance
Lightning Source LLC
Chambersburg PA
CBHW030141170426
43199CB00008B/158